Also by Daniel Blakeslee

The Leader Code

El Codigo Lider

Lead like Hell is Real

Dumping Debt with Online Income

PageCrafters: The Origins of Online Marketing

LEAD
ON
PURPOSE
Tools for Leadership

DANIEL BLAKESLEE

Published by Preacher Books Publishing
2705 Taylor Road, Chesapeake, VA 23321
www.preacherbooks.com

Printed in the United States of America
FIRST EDITION

ISBN: 0615744508
ISBN-13: 978-0615744506

For all of the first time leaders who have built up the courage to delegate for the first time; who nervously wait to see if there is going to be pushback. Especially for those who have been called to lead while serving in the United States Military. You make me proud.

Table of Contents

ACKNOWLEDGMENTS

This book would not have been possible without the countless hours of research performed by my undergraduate students at Baptist Bible College in Springfield, Missouri and my online graduate students at Baptist University of America. The concepts in this book are built upon the work of great researchers who have gone before me, most notably David C. McClelland, Spencer Johnson and Kenneth Blanchard. The first part of this book is the complete second edition of *The Leader Code*. This work could not have been refined were it not for all those who gave me feedback from the first edition.

THE LEADER CODE
Part 1

THE NEW JOB

Christopher stirs as the sun penetrates his eyelids, cutting through a slit in the blinds like a laser. He mouths without any sound coming out, *Note to self: Adjust the blinds before bed tonight.* He then starts to roll over and go back to sleep. After all, he spent the whole weekend unpacking and settling into this big new house. It was at that moment that he remembered the reason they are in this new house: 'because of his new job. *Whoa...today's Monday, isn't it? What time is it?* With eyes completely open now, he struggles to focus on the clock. It's flashing 12:00 pm!

Now wide-awake, adrenaline pumping through his entire body, he immediately realizes he has overslept on the first day at his new job. This is going to be a very bad day!

Christopher is a gifted engineer—so gifted that he made a meteoric rise through the company. He and his wife, Danielle, relocated to Springfield because he was given his own division. This is a tremendous opportunity. He is in the enviable—and many times uncomfortable—position of transitioning from cubicle dweller to leader of a team.

Christopher virtually ran through the shower and jumped into his clothes. Danielle used the Keurig coffeemaker and handed him a cup on the way out the door. He calculated that he could still make it to work on time; all he had to do was break the land speed record. Still, he figures he may not be noticed if he can get there just a *little* late.

Backing out of the driveway, he realized he might have neglected to check that the road was clear as an old beater came driving down the street. An old man driving like an old lady was driving the old car. Christopher stopped just short of hitting the car as the old man swerved to avoid him. Christopher jumped in behind the old man, but he was barely driving the speed limit. He followed him all the way out of the neighborhood to the on-ramp. Christopher thought, *Now's my chance to get ahead of him.* He passed him on the ramp and got into the lane of traffic just ahead of him. Christopher calculated he could still make it only moderately late if he could do 9 mph over the speed limit. His hopes were dashed when he saw traffic creeping along.

He finally made it to his exit. After running the stop sign, he made his way into the parking lot. With no time to look for his reserved parking spot he took the first open one he could find. He jumped out of his car and raced to the front door. As he was getting ready to cross the street, another employee also arriving late caught him off guard. *Wouldn't you know it; it's the old man from the neighborhood.* He waves at Christopher as he cruised by. Christopher thought, *Was that a sarcastic wave? Did he even recognize me or is he just being polite?* No time to analyze now!

Christopher makes it through the security guard by showing the temporary pass he received in the mail. He makes his way up to the third floor and finds his new office. Unfortunately there are three people waiting in his office. He raced past his administrative assistant, who he had never met before. She was trying to warn him about the people waiting to meet with him. The only words he caught from her were "plant manager."

Christopher introduces himself and meets the plant manager, his assistant and a union representative. The meeting starts out with a whole list of problems with the latest design, but Christopher was not even sure what they were referencing. He hoped that fact did not show on his face. Two minutes into the meeting and Christopher thought they were talking like Charlie Brown's teacher. This is going to be a very bad day!

After two more impromptu meetings and many introductions, Christopher finally got a break. He called home to check on Danielle's day. She started filling him in about all the problems with the utility companies. Everything started running together in his mind. All he can think is, *I've got to get organized or this thing is going to eat me alive.*

The next day started out much better. Christopher's alarm clock goes off on time. The blinds are completely closed, so there's no sunshine in his eyes. He gets up early enough to go for a run. He catches up to one of his neighbors out for a jog. Christopher is completely taken aback when he realizes it is the old man that drives the beater like an old lady.

Christopher greets the man with, "Good morning. Great day for a jog."

The old man replied, "It certainly is. I'm Bob. I've wanted to meet you. We actually work together."

Christopher, more than a little embarrassed, said, "Yes, yesterday was my first day and I was running behind. Everything that could go wrong did go wrong."

Bob asked curiously, "So, you had a bad first day?"

"Let's just say I may be in over my head. I've been an engineer my entire adult life, but I've never been in charge of anything or anybody but myself. I am pretty good about managing my own projects, but I have never had to lead people. Heck, I'm not even sure I *like* people." Christopher confesses.

"I know how you feel, I worked my way up from the same cubicle you did. Back when I started with the company, they thought that if you were a good engineer, you were automatically a good leader,"

Bob shared. He went on to explain, "Back then we were left on our own to figure out how to lead and manage people. We've come a long way since then. We now have a great mentoring program for new leaders."

> **Leaders are not born, they are taught; in fact leadership skills are more caught than even taught**

Anxiously, Christopher said, "I think I vaguely remember reading that in the packet I received from the company. However, I just thought that was typical corporate speak. So, you think the mentoring program is helpful?"

"Absolutely! Leaders are not born, they are taught; in fact leadership skills are more caught than even taught. I would be happy to be your leadership mentor if you would allow me," Bob offers graciously. "In fact, if you would allow me, I would love to share with you the Leader Code that I discovered in an ancient Book."

"That would be awesome!" Christopher replied excitedly.

Bob said, "Why don't you come see me this morning after you get settled in at work? My office is on the top floor."

THE ANCIENT BOOK

Christopher got into the office with plenty of time to spare. Fortunately there was no one waiting for him this morning. However, as he prepares to enter the outer office he realized he doesn't remember his administrative assistant's name. *Was it Mary or Maria...? Why can't I remember it? I know I heard her say it.*

"Good morning, Christopher. How are you doing this bright sunny morning?" Christopher's unnamed secretary said cheerfully.

"Well good morning to you, too!" Christopher quickly glances down at her desk plate that says her name is *Marla*. "Is your day off to a good start, Marla?"

Marla replied, "It is. You have two meetings this morning, and then your afternoon is open." Marla hesitated a little then said, "Might I recommend you take that opportunity to meet some of the engineers in the division?"

"No, I have other plans this afternoon. Do you know a guy named Bob that works on the top floor?" Christopher replied sharply.

Marla stopped for a minute, and then said, "The only office on the top floor is our vice president, Bob Tuttle."

Christopher gulped hard. He thinks to himself, *The old guy is Bob, and Bob is my vice president. That actually makes sense.* Then he asked Marla, "50-year-old guy, in good shape with graying temples?"

"That's him. Great guy. He goes by the book, but he is full of grace!"

Christopher sat through his morning meetings. People were still sounding like Charlie Brown's teachers. "Wahhh wah wahhhhh wahhhhhhh wahhh..." Christopher asked himself, *Are these meetings really necessary?*

It appeared people who came to him had only problems. *Doesn't anybody have solutions around here?* He took some time to ponder the issues that were raised this morning. It seemed to Christopher as though these people ought to be able to solve their own problems. After all, that's what he did and that got him promoted to this position.

After a quick lunch in the cafeteria, Christopher grabbed his iPad and headed to the elevator. He looked at the button for the top floor and instead of a number it said "Executive Suite."

He headed up to the top floor, and as he gets off the elevator, Bob himself greets him. Bob is all smiles with an outstretched hand. As they walked, Bob welcomed Christopher to his office and offered him a cup of coffee or a bottle of water. He then introduced him to his administrative assistant Wendy. Bob instructed Wendy to hold his calls until they finish their meeting.

Christopher opened by saying, "I need to apologize. I had no idea you were the vice president. I should have recognized your voice from my phone interview. I should have..."

Bob interrupted, "Would it have made any difference if you knew I was your boss? How would you have treated me differently? Hmm, I hope not at all." Bob continued, "Let's get down to business. I want to share with you the Leader Code I discovered. It has made a tremendous difference in my ability to lead and manage people, projects and this company."

> **Would it have made any difference if you knew I was your boss? How would you have treated me differently?**

Christopher, still in shock that the vice president wants to help him become a better leader, asked curiously, "Yes, you mentioned that this code is from an ancient book?"

Bob explained, "Well, it is actually from the best-selling Book of all time. Have you ever read the Bible?"

Christopher stutters a little, "I'm not really a religious person. I heard stories from the Bible when I was a kid in Sunday school."

Bob said, trying to relieve Christopher's fears, "That's okay—I'm not religious either."

Christopher replied, almost interrupting, "But I don't actually believe the Bible is a 'special' book or even true." Christopher stopped, hoping he hasn't said the wrong thing.

Bob stopped and pondered this for a moment, and then he thoughtfully said, "I understand. One does not have to believe everything in the Bible in order for it to have an impact on one's life." Christopher listened carefully as Bob continued. "For example, the Old Testament part of the Bible contains sanitary guidelines that were written by Moses, who grew up in Egypt. We know from history that Egypt at the time of Moses didn't have a clue about proper sanitary procedures. During the 19th century, a Hungarian obstetrician, Ignaz Philipp Semmelweis, was an assistant professor on the maternity ward of the Vienna General Hospital. He observed that women examined by student doctors who had not washed their hands after leaving the autopsy room had very high death rates. He ordered students to wash their hands with chlorinated lime before examining patients; as a result, the maternal death rate was reduced from 12% to 1% in two years. We have an understanding of germs in the 21st century, but the Bible explained this long before science understood. Modern principles of sanitation were being practiced by the Israelites thousands of years before scientists like Louis Pasteur demonstrated that most infectious diseases were caused by microorganisms originating from outside the body."

Christopher thought about that example for a moment, and then said, "I see. So even if I reject the principles of God and Jesus that I was taught as a child, there are still some ideas that I can learn from the Bible."

"That's right. I'm not trying to convert you, but there are great leadership truths taught in the Bible. These truths, that I call the Leader Code, can help you become a great leader. It would, however, be helpful for you to accept that the Bible is a historically accurate Book. Let me read part of this article to you:

Biblical Data Is Historically Testable

The Bible has become a significant source book for secular archaeology, helping to identify such ancient figures as Sargon (Isaiah 20:1); Sennacherib (Isaiah 37:37); Horam of Gazer (Joshua 10:33); Hazar (Joshua 15:27); and the nation of the Hittites (Genesis 15:20). The biblical record, unlike other "scriptures," is historically set, opening itself up for testing and verification.

Two of the greatest 20th-century archaeologists, William F. Albright and Nelson Glueck, both lauded the Bible (even though they were non-Christian and secular in their training and personal beliefs) as being the single most accurate source document from history. Over and over again, the Bible has been found to be accurate in its places, dates, and records of events. No other "religious" document comes even close.

The 19th-century critics used to deny the historicity of the Hittites, the Horites, the Edomites, and various other peoples, nations, and cities mentioned in the Bible. Those critics have long been silenced by the archaeologist's spade, and few critics dare to question the geographical and ethnological reliability of the Bible.

The names of over 40 different kings of various countries mentioned in the Bible have all been found in contemporary documents and inscriptions outside of the Old Testament and are always consistent with the times and places associated with them in the Bible. Nothing exists in ancient literature that has been even remotely as well confirmed in accuracy, as has the Bible.[1]

"Now, I don't expect you to remember all that information. I've read it many times before and I don't get it all, but I'm an engineer not a historian. The point is that we can learn from the pages of the Bible ideas and principles that can make our life easier."

Christopher's head was spinning. Was his boss asking him to trust the Bible as truth? Or was he just

---

[1] Institute for Creation Research.
http://www.icr.org/bible-history/ (accessed December 12, 2012) and September 11, 2014.

suggesting that he could learn leadership principles from its 'historical' stories? He decided the only thing Bob was asking him to trust was that it worked for him. Obviously Bob had become a successful leader.

"What have I got to lose?" Christopher said to his boss. "Teach me, Obi-Wan."

"Huh?" Bob replied with a puzzled look on his face. Secretly he smiled to himself and thought, *A Star Wars reference; this one is going to be fun.*

"Never mind, just an inside joke," Christopher added sheepishly.

THE FIRST MEETING

Christopher and Bob agreed to meet every morning for breakfast before going into the office. Bob wanted time to explain the principles revealed in the Leader Code that he had discovered in the Bible. Then he wanted Christopher to work on the principles, observe the code in action and report back on what he learned. Bob gave Christopher a copy of the Bible he had in his office. He told Christopher it was not necessary for him to read the entire Book, but it wouldn't hurt either. Christopher decided to read only what was necessary to learn the Leader Code.

This morning Christopher arrived right on time. In fact he arrived before Bob, so he secured a corner booth at the back of the restaurant. Christopher paged through his new Bible and thought to himself, *There are more words in this book than some of my college textbooks. I am very glad Bob did not expect*

· *me to read the whole book.* He looked up to see Bob walking through the front of the restaurant greeting the servers. *I guess he's been here before,* he thought.

"Good morning!" Bob exclaimed.

Christopher returned the greeting then said, "I am really anxious to get started, so what's the first lesson?"

"Listen," is all Bob said.

"Okay, I'm listening."

Bob chuckled and said, "That's your first lesson."

Christopher looked a little confused and replied, "What is?"

"Listen," Bob said again. "The first lesson you need to learn in order to become an effective leader is to listen."

"But I already know how to listen," Christopher said looking confused. "My mother taught me that by the time I was two or three years old. I know that because I became very familiar with Mr. Paddle."

"Do you really know how to listen or do you just know how to hear?"

"Is there a difference?"

Bob looked like he was waiting for that question. "Absolutely. Anyone can hear what is being said, but to really communicate you must listen. For example, my doctor knows how to listen. When I go to see him, he will always ask me why I came in or what's wrong with me. Most people hear a response to that kind of question, but they don't actually listen to the answer. My doctor will listen intently so that he can diagnose my ailment. I learned that listening can help me diagnose a situation so I may lead effectively."

"Now I see the difference, but are you telling me that the Bible talks about listening?" Christopher questioned.

Bob replied without missing a beat. "It sure does. In James 1:19 it says,

My dear brothers, take note of this: Everyone should be quick to listen, slow to speak and slow to become angry.

My grandmother always said, ''God gave us two ears and one mouth so we ought to listen twice as much as we speak.' I think listening is a lost art. Too many leaders believe they have all the answers, but I think those closest to the problem have the ability to figure out a solution. Sometimes they just need a good listener to put their thoughts all together."

> Too many leaders believe they have all the answers, but I think those closest to the problem have the ability to figure out a solution

"I was just thinking the other day that my subordinates ought to be able to solve their own problems instead of coming to me. It seems most of my meetings are just a forum for them to explain their problems."

Bob listened thoughtfully and then countered, "I think you are partially right. However, I look at meetings as a chance for my people to voice their concerns and to work together to solve the challenges. My job, as the leader, is to direct the flow of the meeting so that we don't have a meeting just to say 'we had a meeting'. We will talk more about this later. For now, let's just focus on listening for understanding. Have you listened to what I have said so far? Do you actually understand what we've discussed? Will you remember this information a week from now? A month down the road or next year?"

As that sank in, Bob pulled a couple of books out of his messenger bag. He explained, "In addition to the Bible, there are a few more books I recommend you read."

Christopher jumped in with, "I learned a long time ago when your boss 'recommends' you do something, you sure as heck better do it."

"Well, I'm not your boss now. I am your coach, but the same applies. If your coach recommends something, just do it."

Bob gave him *Tools for Leadership*, by Daniel Blakeslee; *Drive: The Surprising Truth about What Motivates Us*, by Daniel Pink; and *The 5 Levels of Leadership*, by John C. Maxwell. "Read these as you have time, and let me know when you finish. Have you read any books in the *One-Minute Manager* series?"

"Yes, several."

"Terrific," replied Bob. "I believe those are foundational."

Christopher took the hint and took out his iPad and started taking notes. Bob took a legal pad out of his briefcase and laid it on top of the iPad. "Try this," Bob said, "I find actually writing on paper is much more tactile and therefore helps you remember what you write down."

Christopher had a puzzled look on his face and thought, *Really? Pen and paper? Isn't that a little low tech for a couple of high-tech engineers?*

Understanding Christopher's puzzled look, Bob quickly inserted, "Trust me, young Skywalker."

THE CODE

Bob and Christopher were both anxious to get into the Leader Code, but their server interrupted their humorous moment. They quickly looked over the menu, but they already knew what they were going to order.

The men placed their order and the server hurried off to get their breakfast started. Just as Christopher was getting ready to ask another question about listening, Bob interrupted. "We'll apply the idea of listening along the way; let's get into the code."

He continued, "Let me explain the Leader Code I discovered in the Bible...

"There are three Greek words that are used to describe a leader in the New Testament. These words are translated into English in a variety of ways, depending on the context. The words are *poimen,* pronounced *poy-mane,* which means pastor or shepherd; *episkopos,* pronounced *ep-is'-kop-os,* which means bishop or overseer; and *presbuteros,* pronounced *pres-boo'-ter-os,* which means elder."

"Once I discovered these three Greek words are translated to describe a leader in different situations, I went looking for Bible passages that use two or three of these words together."

"Wait a minute," Christopher said. "I am not sure I understand how this can apply to one person or one leader. When I was a kid in church, weren't these titles for three different leaders in a church?" Christopher asked.

"That's probably true," answered Bob. "However, I don't think this teaches a certain form of church government, but instead how those people are to lead. Let me explain." The apostle Peter, who was also an elder, admonished elders in their work:

1 Peter 5:1-3 So I exhort the elders (*presbuteros*) **among you, as a fellow elder and a witness of the sufferings of Christ, as well as a partaker in the glory that is going to be revealed: shepherd the flock** (this is the verb form of the noun *Poimen*) **of God that is among you, exercising oversight** (*episkopos*)**, not under compulsion, but willingly, as God would have you; not for shameful gain, but eagerly; not domineering over those in your charge, but being examples to the flock.**

"We learn that elders (*presbuteros*) are to serve as 'overseers' by having oversight (*episkopos*) as they shepherd (*poimen*) the flock.

"Look at Titus 1:5-7, that's way back here in your Bible:

This is why I left you in Crete, so that you might put what remained into order, and appoint elders *(presbuteros)* in every town as I directed you—if anyone is above reproach, the husband of one wife, and his children are believers and not open to the charge of debauchery or insubordination. For an overseer *(episkopos)*, as God's steward, must be above reproach. He must not be arrogant or quick-tempered or a drunkard or violent or greedy for gain.

"First let me say, who could meet those qualifications? I am sure glad we don't have these requirements at our company," chuckled Christopher. "I will concede your point. These three words seem to be synonymous or at least talking about the same person."

> Elders (*presbuteros*) are to serve as overseers by having oversight (*episkopos*) as they shepherd (*poimen*) the flock

"Let me show you one more passage and then I will explain in detail how the Leader Code works to make us better leaders. Look here in Acts 20, first at verse 17, then down in verse 28."

Now from Miletus he sent to Ephesus and called the elders *(presbuteros)* of the church to come to him.

Pay careful attention to yourselves and to all the flock (derivative of *poimen*), in which the

Holy Spirit has made you overseers *(episkopos)*, **to care for the church of God, which he obtained with his own blood.**

Christopher looked deep in thought as though he were formulating an important question, then he asked, "That last line says 'to care for the Church of God,' but we work at a profit-making company. How does this apply to leadership in our situation?"

"That's a terrific question. I had the same question when I was trying to decipher the code. What I discovered is that if this leadership method works in an organization as complex as a church, then surely it will work in a profit-making company like ours." Bob finished by saying, "And in my years of experience it does work wonderfully."

Bob took out his own legal pad and pen, and then started explaining, "I believe each of these words describes what I like to call a leadership drawer. In each drawer are various tools used to lead others." Unable to determine if Christopher fully understood, Bob asked, "Do you have a toolbox?"

"Of course, I'm an engineer. I like to tinker."

Bob continued, "Think of these three Greek words as a drawer in your toolbox. In your toolbox you have various drawers that are designed to hold certain tools. You probably have a flat drawer near the top that is perfect for screwdrivers, a bigger drawer with double slides at the bottom that is best to hold hammers and heavy tools and maybe even a square drawer that works well for bulky items like chains.

"These drawers are designed to hold tools you can use to lead or influence others. Since individuals are unique, what motivates them or drives them, as Daniel Pink puts it in his book *Drive: The Surprising Truth about what Motivates Us*[2], is intrinsic. Pink says, "That first drive (Motivation 1.0) didn't fully account for who we are. We also had a second drive—to seek rewards and avoid punishment more broadly.[3]"

"However, Pink goes on to say, "'To help your employees find autonomy, the best strategy for an employer would be to figure out what's important to each individual employee.'[4]"

"I define each of these drawers by how it drives people, both leaders and followers. The tools in the *poimen* drawer work best with people who are driven to get the task completed. They are motivated by achieving a task or as I like to say, **Task First**. The leaders who primarily use this drawer are what John Maxwell in his book *The 5 Levels of Leadership*, calls level one leaders.[5] They rely upon their positional authority. People follow them because they have the position or title.

"It is logical for someone to start their leadership journey when they are assigned their first leadership position. One day someone transfers or moved out and all of a sudden you are given a title. This is

---

[2] Daniel Pink, *Drive: The Surprising Truth about What Motivates Us*, (New York: Penguin Books, 2011).

[3] Ibid., p. 16.

[4] Ibid., p. 106.

[5] John C. Maxwell, "The 5 Levels of Leadership," (New York: Center Street, 2011). p. 7.

when we reach into that *poimen* drawer. We are relying on that title or position to influence others.

"What was your first leadership position?"

Christopher thought for a moment before responding. It looked like he had to reach back into the deep recess of his memory. Then he offered, "It would have to be back in high school. I was flipping burgers evenings and weekends. After about a year on the job, which was a long time by comparison to the other employees, my manager made me the line supervisor."

"How did that work out for you?"

"Not so great," Christopher responded sheepishly. "I was pretty ineffective. I thought that everyone would just do what I said because I was the line supervisor. I was really good at the job, so I thought everyone would want to do what I told them. I was shocked to find out they were not as excited as I was to learn the job and work hard at it. It was a valuable learning experience."

"Would you be surprised to hear that is typical of a new supervisor? You make mistakes in leadership and learn from them, and then you put what you learned in your drawer so you will know better next time. Other times you have success and you learn what works and you save that in your drawer too.

Christopher was nodding his head now. He offered an example to show he listened to understand. "So it's like making a leadership deposit in a leadership bank. You make deposits and withdrawals in your leadership drawer as you interact with people?"

"I like that illustration. I think it works well here." Bob continued, "When you get your first leadership position, usually your title or position is the only thing in your drawer. Using your illustration, your account only has the minimum required balance. In you leadership toolbox, your title will be the only tool you have available and what you depend on to influence others.

"The *poimen* drawer is the starting place for every level of leadership. As Maxwell puts it, position is the bottom floor—the foundation upon which leadership must be built.[6]

"One example from the Bible of someone who operated out of their *poimen* drawer was King Saul. Saul led using his title as King of Israel. You mentioned that you heard Bible stories in Sunday school when you were a child. Do you remember hearing any about King Saul?"

Christopher nodded his head, "Yes, as a matter of fact I do. I am actually surprised that I remember him. He was the first king of Israel, wasn't he?"

"Very good. I like to use him as an example of a leader who depended on his *poimen* drawer because many have either read or at least heard about King Saul somewhere along the way. He was a King who was good in most respects. That is, until he started messing up. When he started depending on his title to lead the people. That is when his leadership became ineffective."

Bob opened up his Bible to 1 Samuel 10:24 and then helped Christopher find it in his. Then he read,

And Samuel said to all the people, "Do you see him whom the Lord has chosen? There is none

---

[6] Ibid. p. 39

like him among all the people." And all the people shouted, "Long live the king!"

"What do you think would happen to you if you didn't shout 'Long live the king'? If a man had the title of king, you better bow down. His title was the only thing that mattered.

"My first leadership experience is not too different from yours," Bob said. "I was made captain of my high school wrestling team. I had a title and a nice letter C to put on my uniform, but very little influence over my teammates. I found I could get them to follow me some of the time, usually if it was something they wanted to do anyway, but other times I had to 'pull rank' on them. When I pulled rank, I was basically making them shout, 'Long live the captain.' They did what I said, because they knew they could not wrestle if they didn't.

"Daniel Pink equates this to using a 'carrot and a stick' to motivate people. He refers to researchers, such as Harvard Business School's Teresa Amabile, when he concludes, 'External rewards and punishments—both carrots and sticks—can work nicely for algorithmic tasks. But they can be devastating for heuristic ones.[7] Since we work with engineers trying to solve problems that currently have no solutions, the carrot and stick method of motivation can be, as stated, devastating.

"Remember, your followers also have something that drives them. You will have subordinates whose drive comes from the *poimen* drawer. These are usually really hard workers who are task-oriented.

---

[7] Pink, *p. 28.*

Remember people with *poimen* drive are **Task First**. Pink's research shows that people like this have great internal motivation that we could stifle if we don't recognize it.[8]

"When we get tasked with a leadership role or promoted to a leadership position with a shiny new title, a certain amount of authority or influence usually comes with it. Most of the time, as with both of us, that influence is very limited."

Christopher interrupted, "But not everyone fails as a new leader. I have experienced many new supervisors who did a remarkable job. I followed them willingly, not just because I had to because of their new title. They were good at what they did and I liked them."

> If you believe that a title makes you a leader then... the only thing in your drawer will be your title and you will find the other drawers are locked up tight

"Very true, but you are getting a little ahead of me. Most times when someone gets that new promotion or title, it's because they deserved it. They have already been effective at their job and may already have the respect of their co-workers. Obviously their boss or supervisor saw something they liked or they would not have promoted them. The Bible explains this in Luke 12:48b:

---

[8] Ibid.

...to whom much was given, of him much will be required, and from him to whom they entrusted much, they will demand the more.

"When you get that promotion, it is important to use your new authority wisely. You should use your position to improve the team, to accomplish the organization's mission and to help the people you are leading. You want to ensure you use what is in your *poimen* drawer in the appropriate amounts. If you open your drawer judiciously, the people will begin to give you greater authority. When that happens, you gain influence, not just because of your title. This is when you start adding deposits to your drawer.

"However, if you believe that a title makes you a leader, then you will have a hard time becoming a good leader. The only thing in your drawer will be your title and you will find the other drawers are locked up tight.

"So," Bob reminded Christopher, "these are three Greek words that are used to describe a leader. We can use them to identify drawers in our leadership toolbox. We have talked about *poimen;* remember it means pastor or shepherd. Then we have *episkopos,* which means bishop or overseer and *presbuteros,* which means elder."

"So, let me see if I got this. The code reveals to us three different leadership drawers and we just pick one and take out the tools that seem appropriate. Does that pretty much sum it up?" naïvely asked Christopher.

"No, we have not even scratched the surface. I have much to teach you my young apprentice," Bob said in his best Yoda imitation.

Christopher made some quick notes, so he wouldn't forget what he had learned.

CHRISTOPHER'S NOTEBOOK

The three internal drives people are based on three Greek words in the New Testament of the Bible. These words are used to describe a leader. These words are translated into English a few different ways. The words are **Poimen** pronounced *poy-mane'* which means pastor or shepherd, **Episkopos** pronounced *ep-is'-kop-os,* which means bishop or overseer and **Presbuteros** pronounced *pres-boo'-ter-os* that means elder.

The drives are **Poimen, Episkopos,** and **Presbuteros.**

THE TOOLBOX

The next meeting could not come fast enough for Christopher. He shared all that he had learned with Danielle and even she shared his excitement. He knew she would enjoy discussing what he learned about drive and motivation. All that psychological stuff was right up her alley. She loved hearing about theories of how people thought and behaved. She was also thrilled that her husband was bonding with someone from work and adjusting well.

Bob and Christopher pulled into the parking lot at the same time. Christopher looked over at Bob's car and wanted to ask him why a person in his position drove such a beater, but he thought better of it. *Maybe another time.*

Once they were seated and put their order in, Bob reviewed some of what they had discussed up to this point.

He took out his handwritten notes that looked like they had been through the wringer and checked to make sure he didn't miss anything. He finished his review by going over what they discussed about the drawers.

"The three drawers are defined by how they drive people. We've already gone over the first drawer, the *poimen* drawer, and we remember the tools in it work best with people who are driven to get the task completed. They are motivated primarily by **task accomplishment**.

"These leaders are level one leaders[9] according to John Maxwell in his book *The 5 Levels of Leadership*. They rely upon their positional authority. People follow them because they have a position or title."

Bob retrieved the graph that he had drawn on his legal pad. He pointed to the words as he spoke about the specific drawer. Christopher followed his lead and located his drawing of the graph. He knew it was going to come in handy.

"The other two drawers are *presbuteros* and *episkopos*. They too contain what drives us. I think I read this quote from Daniel Pink before but it bears repeating here, 'Human beings have an innate inner drive to be autonomous, self-determined, and connected to one another. And when that drive is liberated, people achieve more and live richer lives.'[10] One thing to notice about what he said is that we have an 'innate inner drive.'

---

[9] John C. Maxwell, *The 5 Levels of Leadership*, p. 7.
[10] Pink, *p. 26.*

"These drives are the needs, or wants, that are related to our goals. What drives us determines our thoughts. Our thoughts impact our behaviors, or as the Bible says it in Luke 6:45,

The good person out of the good treasure of his heart produces good, and the evil person out of his evil treasure produces evil, for out of the abundance of the heart his mouth speaks.

Our behavior or our actions lead us to accomplish our goals. Let me diagram the relationship of drive to goals:

DRIVE -> THOUGHT -> BEHAVIOR -> GOAL ACCOMPLISHMENT

"There are physiological drives such as hunger or thirst. Pink calls this Motivation 1.0.[11] We also know there are intellectual drives like curiosity; but when dealing with the Leader Code, we are focusing on the drive contained in our three drawers: *poimen*, *presbuteros* and *episkopos*.

"So for *poimen,* the drive is to put the **Task First.**

"Then, inside the *presbuteros* drawer is the drive to put **People First.**

"And inside the *episkopos* drawer is the drive to put the **Mission First**."

"Well, can't you want all three of these?" interrupted Christopher.

---

[11] Ibid. p. 10.

"You can have all three of these drives, but only one can be first. Think about it: since these drives lead to thoughts and then behaviors, one or more of these drives could lead someone to act contrary to the others. One of them has to win out."

"That makes sense, please go on. My wife finds this type of discussion fascinating, so I will have something more to discuss tonight."

DRIVE leads to

THOUGHTS lead to

BEHAVIOR leads to

GOAL ACCOMPLISHMENT

"As you may know, or at least your wife knows, there has been a great deal of research on drive and motivation. Some of it is cited by Pink in his book, but there are many other books and articles on this topic—far more than a couple of engineers can digest and discuss intelligently."

Bob took out his pad again and started to make a list of seven items. "I guess the bottom line of much of that research is summarized in several points:

1. As leaders, we need to understand that normal, healthy adults have potential energy stored in their 'toolboxes.'

2. Adults, not just leaders, have access to the three drawers; they can reach into any of the drawers and draw out some potential energy from storage.

3. Adults vary widely in the size of their drawers. Therefore, some will have more energy stored in

their *poimen* drawer than someone else might have, and so on.

4. Whether one of the drives manifests itself into thoughts and behaviors or not depends on the specific situation in which the person finds him- or herself.

5. The specific circumstances of a situation can trigger a different drive. Each drawer will open in response to a different set of situational circumstances.

6. Since the three drawers are directed toward different kinds of goals, i.e., Task, People or Mission, the behavior that results from arousal of a drive is quite distinct for each one. In other words, each drive leads to a distinct pattern of behavior.

7. When the circumstances of a situation change, a different drawer can be opened and a different drive can be aroused, resulting in different patterns of behavior."

BEHAVIOR = DRIVE X SITUATION

"Well then," Christopher asked carefully searching for the right words, "does that mean that a person's behavior is a product of both their drive, specifically how much is in each drawer and the situations they find themselves in?"

Bob replied, "I believe so. The toolbox drawers are a set size and we have a certain amount of each drive, but the variable is the situation. For example, when your job changes you are in a different situation. Your behaviors will be different, not because your drive has changed, but because the situation has changed."

"So in engineer terms:

$$BEHAVIOR = DRIVE \times SITUATION$$

"Since D, or drive is a constant, you can solve for B, or behavior, by observing how S, or how the situation, has changed."

Bob looked surprised and said, "The force is strong with this one!"

Bob waived the server over to top off their cups. Both of them needed a break from the psychology lesson. This is too much soft science for engineers who were used to dealing with measurable data.

After some small talk for a few minutes, Bob got back to his explanation. "Not everyone agrees where our drive or motivations come from, but I believe that drive is developed in childhood and generally remains unchanged with everything else being equal. Therefore, if a situation is neutral, a person's natural drive will determine his or her behavior.

"As we already said, situations impact thoughts and concerns that will cause a person to open up a different drawer. For example, if a person goes to a party where there are many interesting and friendly people, he or she is likely to respond with *presbuteros* behaviors: people first. If a person works in a job or for a leader and receives no responsibility, opportunity to perform better or feedback on performance, this individual is unlikely to demonstrate *poimen* behaviors."

"And will probably be very frustrated and spend their time surfing the web," interjected Christopher.

They both chuckled and Bob opened up his notepad and grabbed a new pen. Christopher knew this meant he was getting ready to take a lot of notes.

"Let me lay out each of the toolbox drawers for you," Bob started. "It helps to understand what the typical thoughts and behaviors of each drawer would be.

"Starting with the *poimen* drawer: You know a person using this drawer is driven or motivated by **Task First**. They think about outperforming other people at work and about meeting their self-imposed standards of excellence. They will think about offering unique contributions to a project, while also thinking about advancing their career.

> **Leaders, who depend on the poimen drawer, generally put the task first**

"Of course these thoughts will lead to behaviors like setting goals for themselves and looking forward to getting feedback about how they are doing on the job. Since they want to offer something unique to a project, they will frequently take initiative and be innovative. However, they will take personal responsibility if things go wrong.

"Another behavior frequently found in people using their *poimen* drawer is that they will hang out with experts over friends. They would rather work with someone who knows what they're doing than someone they like personally."

"Wow, is that what I'm doing, hanging out with an expert?" Christopher quipped.

"Well, I guess that depends; are you saying you don't like me personally?"

"No, that's not what I meant. I was trying to make a joke. It just didn't..."

"Yep, me too. Except mine was funnier. I just wish I had a picture of the look on your face!"

"Sure, laugh at my expense."

"Well, moving on," Bob continued. "Inside the *presbuteros* drawer is the drive to put **People First**. They think about developing close friendships and maintaining those friendships even in the workplace. They think

> **Leaders, who depend on the presbuteros drawer, generally put people first**

about hanging out with others just to enjoy their company, like I do with you." Bob smirked as Christopher caught the reference, but as he was getting ready to respond Bob continued with, "When they are separated from others, they have concern and they want to restore those relationships as soon as possible. Whenever there is a group activity, they will see it as a social occasion.

"These thoughts will lead to behaviors like having many friends, talking to or texting others frequently—even to people at work during working hours. That means they will sometimes use business email for personal correspondence and probably make a lot of phone calls. The calls may be work-related, but they will end up being more personal in nature.

"This person would rather work with other people than be alone, because they put people before the task. That means they will usually choose friends to work with over experts. It is important for this person to gain personal approval from coworkers and supervisors.

"They will tend to communicate in terms of how others think and feel. Which means they are prone to empathize, sympathize, and console their coworkers. They could end up being a sounding board for others, even disgruntled employees.

"Coffee?"

"Yes, just one more cup, just let me finish getting that last part down."

The server came by with a fresh pot of coffee at just the right time and Bob caught his second wind. "The leaders who primarily use the *presbuteros* drawer are what John Maxwell calls level two leaders.[12] They rely upon their relationships with their subordinates to lead. People follow them because they know, like and trust them.

"This drawer is about people and putting them first. I will show you the behaviors that come out of this drawer and you will see that it is used to build relationships. Building relationships builds a foundation for influencing others. The more that authority barriers come down and relationships are

---

[12] John C. Maxwell, "The 5 Levels of Leadership," p. 8.

strengthened; the stronger the foundation for leading others.

"One leader in the Bible was Joshua; he literally broke down barriers, but that event is not what I am referring to. Do you remember him from your Sunday school days?"

Christopher thought for a moment then responded, "Sure, isn't he the one with the coat of many colors?"

"No, that was Joseph and we'll talk about him later. You may have sung a song about Joshua conquering Jericho. He was with Moses in the desert wondering about with the children of Israel for 40 years."

"That's because they left the men in charge. No real man is going to stop and ask for directions," Christopher chuckled.

Bob smirked and acted as though he had not already heard that joke dozens of times. "As a leader, Joshua was willing to serve. For 40 years he served under Moses in the wilderness. He was known as 'Moses's assistant,' 'his servant'. In Exodus 24:13 it says,

So Moses rose with his assistant Joshua, and Moses went up into the mountain of God.
Then in Exodus 33:11,
Thus the Lord used to speak to Moses face to face, as a man speaks to his friend. When Moses turned again into the camp, his assistant Joshua the son of Nun, a young man, would not depart from the tent.

"Great leaders are people who have no problem with serving others, because it helps prepare them to lead. Even as a leader, Joshua was willing to serve. Though having been exalted by the Lord in Joshua 3:7,

The Lord said to Joshua, 'Today I will begin to exalt you in the sight of all Israel, that they may know that, as I was with Moses, so I will be with you.'

Or in Joshua 4:14

On that day the Lord exalted Joshua in the sight of all Israel, and they stood in awe of him...

"Maxwell says that when people feel liked, cared for, included, valued and trusted, they begin to work together with their leader and each other. That can change the entire working environment. There is an old saying, 'People go along with leaders they get along with.'

"Adding this second drawer is an important development in leadership because this is where followers give their supervisors permission to lead them.[13] People change from being subordinates to being followers for the first time, and that means there is movement. Leadership always means that people are going somewhere. Another old saying is, 'If you are leading and no one is following, you are just taking a walk'.

"Are you still with me?" Bob asked as he tried to get the servers attention for more coffee. "You want some?"

---

[13] Ibid, p. 86.

Christopher nodded that he was still tracking then answered, "Okay, but this has to be the last cup for me. I need to take a quick break."

After they took a restroom break and topped off their cups, Bob moved to the last drawer. "And finally," he said, "inside the *episkopos* drawer is the drive to put the **Mission First**. This person thinks about taking strong and forceful actions and about giving help, advice and support, often unsolicited.

> Leaders, who depend on the episkopos drawer, generally put the mission first

"They also will think about strategies and about how to influence people and direct or control a situation. However, they will think about the impact of their actions and how coworkers will feel or be influenced. Status, reputation, and position are important to them and it will also influence their thoughts.

"These thoughts will manifest themselves in visible behaviors, like being active in organizational politics."

"I already don't like this behavior. I dislike having to deal with office politics," Christopher inserted.

"One thing to consider is that most of the behaviors that come out of our drawers can be positive or negative. It depends on the situation. Remember that is the variable in your equation."

"I forgot that. You cannot really judge until you get the entire picture or equation."

"These next behaviors are the perfect example. These people frequently seek positions of leadership and they influence people through control or persuasion or offers of help or assistance. It is not bad to want to be in charge or influence people if your motives are right. Remember what's driving this person is mission.

"They also tend to train their subordinates and help them improve their task performance, but they will also seek, withhold and use information to influence people. They prefer to be around other people who get things done. That ultimately creates growth for the organization."

With a look of understanding, Christopher commented, "Now, I assume a leader who draws form the *episkopos* drawer is a level three leader according to Maxwell?"

"That would be correct. Maxwell says the five levels are like a building—all the higher levels rest on the lower ones.[14] He also explains that a leader must pass through every level to get to the next one. Level two builds on level one and therefore you can't be a level three leader until you've mastered level two: Permission. Once you've built a relationship with your people, you're ready to focus on producing results. Level three is the Production level. This is where leadership really takes off and goes to another level.[15]

"Level three qualifies and separates true leaders from people who merely occupy leadership

---

[14] Ibid, p. 11.
[15] Ibid, p. 133.

positions. Good leaders always make things happen. They get results. They accomplish the organization's mission. Just as level one was task first and level two was people first, leaders who draw from the *episkopos* drawer put the mission first.

"These leaders can make a significant impact on an organization. Not only are they productive individually, but because they are in charge, they also are able to help the team produce. This ability gives leaders who draw from the *episkopos* drawer confidence, credibility and increased influence. Maxwell says that no one can fake level three.[16] Either you're producing for the organization and getting something done or you're not."

Christopher thoughtfully digested all that he had learned about these three drawers and he stated, half as a question and half as a statement, "Leaders at level one, who use their title from their *poimen* drawer, get to be leaders for many reasons. They may demonstrate potential, they may be connected and they may be good at playing politics. It could be as simple as they have seniority and they were the only ones left. Or they could be like me and just got lucky that the company was desperate." He chuckled as he continued, "If a leader is a people person and they are simply good with people, they tend to draw from the *presbuteros* drawer. I am sure some people go to great lengths to improve their people skills so they can move up to level two and unlock the *presbuteros* drawer.

---

[16] Ibid, p. 133-34.

"But I think there are some leaders who will never be able to draw from the *episkopos* drawer. These leaders will not be able to move up from level two (Permission) to level three (Production)."

"Why do you think that is?" asked Bob sincerely.

"Well, I think it's because they never seem to be able to meet goals. They just can't meet the minimum expectations and produce results." answered Christopher, proud that he knew the answer.

"I think you are right on target. There was a leader in the Bible that you mentioned before. The guy with the 'Technicolor dream coat.'"

"Joseph."

"That is correct. Joseph drew from his *episkopos* drawer. He put the mission first at all cost and produced results. I would say he was clearly a level three leader. If you remember, he led Egypt to store up grain from the seven bountiful years for the seven years of famine.

"When the Egyptian people were hungry, he produced.

"I took on my first leadership role at the company when I was a little younger than you. I only knew how to use my *poimen* drawer. About the only thing in it was my title. I was clearly a level one leader. At least I thought I was the leader of the department, but what I later learned was that one of the engineers in the department was the actual leader. Everyone looked to him for direction. He had all of the influence. I did not have credibility yet. I spent time with the guys in the department. I even visited the homes of key personnel. Soon they began to like and trust me and I was using my *presbuteros* drawer; I had successfully moved to level two.

"I told my wife, 'I need to get some wins under my belt.' Over time, we had some victories when we completed projects on time and under budget. We had several occasions when my workgroup solved major issues for the company and we were praised by the brass. It is true that nothing builds credibility likes success. We started winning and people started following. I was using all three drawers and life was good.

"Soon the other guys in my department started modeling my behavior. They were soon using tools from the other drawers. It came to the point that I could assign any of them to be the lead on a project and I knew I could count on them. They liked winning.

"Think about what you remember about the story of Joseph: sold into slavery by his brothers, trapped and then falsely accused by his boss's wife, thrown into prison and yet he still kept his faith in God. He was an example to Pharaoh's butler in prison and later it paid dividends in Genesis 41:41

Pharaoh said to Joseph, 'See, I have set you over all the land of Egypt.'

"Joseph cast a vision that would save the people from starvation—they bought into his vision. He didn't stop there; he kept the vision before the people. In Genesis 41:45,

Joseph went out over the land of Egypt.

"Joseph solved a problem that would have devastated the nation of Egypt, but he didn't know it would also save his family from starvation and would lead to the Messiah being born from his ancestors.

"There is so much more we could talk about concerning the drawers in our leadership toolbox, but it's going to be lunchtime before we finish breakfast if we don't get into the office. I have another dozen pages of notes, so we can talk about this sometime in the future.

"For now we need to focus on the styles of leadership that are in each drawer. These three drawers will provide you with the tools you need for most of the situations[17] that you will face as a leader. I learned about situational leadership back in college when I read *Management of Organizational Behavior: Utilizing Human Resources*[18] by Paul Hersey and Kenneth Blanchard. Blanchard and Hersey were pioneers in this way of thinking. When I began to study these three words in relationship to the job of the pastor, I realized they actually encompassed the styles or methods by which a person can lead others. That will have to wait for another day."

"Well, it's a good thing I planned ahead and delegated all the tasks out yesterday or I would be in real trouble with my boss for getting into the office this late," Christopher joked.

---

[17] Richard Porter, "Piecing Together a Shattered Church," *Leadership* 9 (Spring 1988): 82-89.

[18] Paul Hersey and Kenneth H Blanchard, Management of Organizational Behavior: Utilizing Human Resources (New Jersey: Prentice Hall Incorporated, 1996).

"Who says you won't be in trouble with your boss?"

THE TOOLS

Christopher went home after work and pondered what Bob had taught him that day. He even opened the Bible and read the verses he had jotted down. In fact he read through them several times. His wife did not ask any questions. She was just happy to see him reading the Bible and she certainly did not want ruin this opportunity.

Without even waiting for the alarm, Christopher rose early the next day. He was excited to get his workday started, and he was especially looking forward to his breakfast meeting. Danielle barely stirred when Christopher went out for his morning jog. She was awake by the time he returned and had coffee ready for him.

Bob pulled into the parking lot just before Christopher. He pulled up next to him and the two men walked into "their" restaurant together. Bob made some comment about carpooling and his comment was met with some disparaging remarks about his car. He was used to people making fun of his old beater. He just told himself, *No car payments*.

The two men made their way to their "regular" booth, ordered breakfast and got right to business. Bob reviewed what they had discussed the previous day and answered a few questions Christopher had thought of the night before. Bob was excited that Christopher had thought through the information enough to ask questions. It was also evident that he had read through the Bible verses.

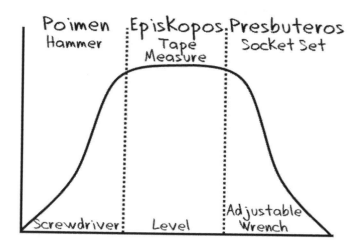

Bob started drawing as he spoke. "The three drawers in your leadership toolbox contain the tools needed in most of the scenarios in which a leader will find him or herself." Bob drew this graph as he explained.

"In each drawer in your leadership toolbox, you will find two leadership styles.

> **Each drawer in the toolbox contains a pair of Leadership Styles**

"In the *poimen* drawer, you will find the Hammer leadership style and the Screwdriver leadership style."

Christopher started to interrupt, but Bob explained, "I know what you're thinking—these are not literal tools. You will get a better understanding of how each tool represents a leadership style as we go on. In this case, a screwdriver is not a tool for tightening fasteners—it is a style of leadership[19] that we use quite frequently in our line of work. But let me finish explaining; I think this will become obvious.

"Next, the *presbuteros* drawer contains the Socket Set leadership style and the Adjustable Wrench leadership style, while the *episkopos* drawer contains the Measuring Tape leadership style and the Bubble Level leadership style."

"I'm going to wait to ask you about the bell curve because I know you're going to get to that, but what's the difference between the top leadership style and the bottom leadership style?"

Bob continued with a knowing look on his face. "I'm glad you asked. Each of these leadership styles

---

[19] Franklin M. Segler, "The Pastor and Church Administration," *Southwestern Journal of Theology* 1 (Winter 1959): 26-34.

can be described in terms of several skills that every leader must have. Each of these skills impact subordinates in some way.

"First, leaders must listen, as we discussed when we first met. Every leader takes input from subordinates in order to diagnose and solve problems. However, each leadership style listens and takes input in a different way.

Second, a leader must provide vision.[20] Every leader sets goals and plans,[21] either long-range or short-range. One place the Bible speaks to this is in Luke 14:28-32.

> **For which of you, desiring to build a tower, does not first sit down and count the cost, whether he has enough to complete it? Otherwise, when he has laid a foundation and is not able to finish, all who see it begin to mock him, saying, 'This man began to build and was not able to finish.' Or what king, going out to encounter another king in war, will not sit down first and deliberate whether he is able with ten thousand to meet him who comes against him with twenty thousand? And if not, while the other is yet a great way off, he sends a delegation and asks for terms of peace.**

---

[20]   Jerry R. Young, "Shepherds, Lead!" *Grace Theological Journal* 6 (Spring 1985): 329-35.

[21]   Jere Allen, "Guiding Churches through Change, Review and Expositor, April 1984, pp. 571-81.

"Each leadership style will set goals, plan and share vision differently.[22]

"The styles will be described in relationship to how each deals with the amount of stress involved, the task and the people involved."

Christopher interrupted again, "I know I'm getting ahead of you, but are you going to define each style by the different ways they do these leadership tasks? Because I think I can fill in some blanks. For example, I bet the Hammer leadership style pounds his people all the time and I don't think I have to tell you what the Screwdriver leadership style does to his people."

"Methinks you are jumping to conclusion, my young apprentice. That is only true depending on the situation," Bob replied with a horrible Yoda imitation. "Remember *poimen* can be translated as "shepherd." What does a shepherd do when the wolves come in to steal sheep? "

"I suppose he beats 'em with that long shepherd's crook that he carries in every Christmas pageant I've seen. I submit to your wisdom. Please go on."

"*Poimen* can also be translated as "pastor" Hopefully a pastor isn't always beating you over the head." Bob continued to explain the leadership tasks.

[22] Don Cousins, Leith Anderson and Arthur DeKruyter, *Mastering Church Management* (Portland, Oregon: Multnomah Press, 1990), p. 18.

"Remember we are talking about the Hammer as a leader[23] and not referring to nails as the followers.

"The next task each leader must perform is delegation. This one is very important for people like us who come out of a field where we are our own boss. Delegation is very important, but more specifically, it's about how one delegates.[24]

"In Exodus 18:17-23 Moses' father in law gave him some clear advice about delegation.[25] He told Moses..."

"Hold on a minute! Moses had a father-in-law? Well, I would never have thought that. Sorry, please continue."

"Yes, his name was Jethro.[26] It says so right here starting in verse 17:

Moses' father-in-law said to him, "What you are doing is not good. You and the people with you will certainly wear yourselves out, for the thing is too heavy for you. You are not able to do it alone. Now obey my voice; I will give you advice, and God be with you! You shall represent the people before God and bring their

---

[23] Kenneth H Blanchard and Spencer Johnson, *The One Minute Manager* (USA: Penguin Group Incorporated, 1985), 31.

[24] James B. Ashbrook, "Creative Church Administration," Pastoral Psychology,   June 1957, pp. 11-16.

[25] Carl F. George, "Recruitment's Missing Link," Leadership 3 (Summer 1982): 54-60.

[26] Joseph S. Exell, "Exodus," *The Biblical Illustrator*, (Grand Rapids: Baker Book House, 1955), p. 319.

cases to God, and you shall warn them about the statutes and the laws, and make them know the way in which they must walk and what they must do. Moreover, look for able men from all the people, men who fear God, who are trustworthy and hate a bribe, and place such men over the people as chiefs of thousands, of hundreds, of fifties, and of tens. And let them judge the people at all times. Every great matter they shall bring to you, but any small matter they shall decide themselves. So it will be easier for you, and they will bear the burden with you. If you do this, God will direct you, you will be able to endure, and all this people also will go to their place in peace."

"Jethro advised Moses to setup a chain of command so he would not burn out from doing all the work himself. I've known many leaders along the way that could have benefited from this small piece of advice."

The server came by and warmed up Bob's coffee. He took a sip, and then looked at his watch. He exclaimed, "I better finish these last two pretty quickly or we're going to be real late getting in again today.

"After delegation, it is important for a leader to praise his or her people. This simply involves giving feedback about the tasks that were delegated and rewarding people for doing a good job.[27] In one of my favorite leadership books, *The One Minute*

---

[27] Frank Damazio, *The Making of a Leader* (Portland, Oregon: Bible Press, 1980), pp. 144-45.

Manager, Kenneth Blanchard says, 'Help people reach their full potential, catch them doing something right.'[28]

"It also means providing negative feedback when the job was not performed as expected.[29] The apostle Paul wrote a couple of letters to the church in Corinth[30] giving them negative feedback about their performance. He said in 2 Corinthians 7: 8,

For even if I made you grieve with my letter, I do not regret it—though I did regret it, for I see that that letter grieved you, though only for a while.

"The final task a leader must perform is what the Bible calls *discipleship*. Discipleship simply means training others. One of the jobs of a leader is to train his replacement; to work himself out of a job.

"Probably the clearest passage of Scripture dealing with discipleship is Matthew 20:18-20:

And Jesus came and said to them, 'All authority in heaven and on earth has been given to me. Go therefore and make disciples of all nations, baptizing them in the name of the Father and of the Son and of the Holy Spirit, teaching them to observe all that I have commanded you. And

---

[28] Blanchard, *The One Minute Manager*, p. 39.

[29] Paul D. Myra and Harold L. Robbins, "Conflict: Facing it in Yourself and Your Church," *Leadership* 1 (February 1980): 23-26.

[30] F. F. Bruce, "First and Second Corinthians," in *The New Century Commentary*, ed. Matthew Black (Grand Rapids: William B. Eardmans Publishing Co., 1971).

behold, I am with you always, to the end of the age.'

"These verses are pretty straightforward, but one small detail that is often overlooked is that the only imperative command in the entire passage is to *'make disciples.'*"

Christopher let out a long sigh and said, "Well, at least you didn't give me as much to remember today as you did yesterday. So, each leadership style is defined by how it performs these tasks:

CHRISTOPHER'S NOTEBOOK

1. Listens to subordinates in order to diagnose and solve problems.

2. Casts vision by setting goals; develop long- and short-term plans.

3. Delegates; directs others to perform tasks.

4. Praises by providing feedback and rewards.

5. Disciples by training and developing others.

Does that summarize it?"

"Great job! I will be out of town until Tuesday. Let's plan to pick it up from here at that time," Bob said as he picked up the check and headed for the door. Apparently he did not want to be as late getting in the office today as he was yesterday.

THE S.T.P.

Over the next several days, Christopher reviewed his notes and tried to monitor how he performed each of the five tasks of a leader. He was so excited about what he was learning that he had to share it with his wife. Danielle didn't really have any interest in the subject, but she was very excited that he was reading the Bible for the first time since she'd known him.

Christopher called Bob's wife, Rose, and asked if he could pick Bob up from the airport. Rose was more than happy to let him fight the traffic. She was also aware that Christopher was her husband's latest disciple and therefore needed more time with Bob.

Christopher passed the time on the drive to the airport by listening to the audio version of *The One Minute Manager*. He arrived at the airport, found the correct gate and waited for Bob holding a sign that said, "Mr. Kenobi." When Bob passed through the TSA secure area, he laughed out loud.

Once they settled into the car and got on the road, Christopher started in right away. "I can't believe I let you get away without telling me what the X- and Y axis were for!"

Bob turned to look at his young apprentice and sarcastically said, "Only an engineer would lose sleep over what should go on the X and Y axis. The X axis is PEOPLE and the Y axis is STRESS. People range from unskilled to skilled. You could probably come up with many different ways to define the type of people you work with, but in our line of work, skilled and unskilled seems to work best. The same could be said for stress. I define stress ranging from low stress to high stress. Other professions may define the Y axis differently. I like using stress because it gives me a nice acronym, STP, which I always used in my cars as a teenager."

Chris said, almost mumbling, "With the kind of cars you drive, you should probably buy stock in STP."

"I also live without car payments, thank you very much," Bob replied triumphantly. Then he continued, "So here is what our graph looks like."

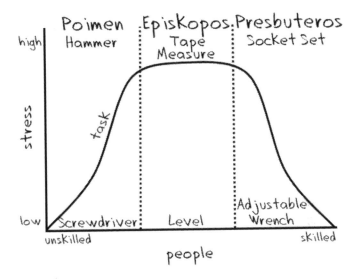

"Again," started Christopher, "maybe it's the engineer in me, but this graph makes perfect sense. When working with unskilled workers in a low-stress scenario, a leader could operate in the Screwdriver leadership style. With those same workers in a high-stress scenario, the leader should transition to a Hammer leadership style. However, if your workers are highly skilled, then using the Socket Set leadership style in a high-stress situation is more appropriate and backing off to the Adjustable Wrench style in low-stress situations. If you have people who are moderately skilled, ideally you would use either the Level leadership style or the Measuring Tape leadership style depending on the level of stress in the situation. That just leaves the bell curve?"

Bob smiled and continued his explanation. "The bell curve is labeled for the actual task being performed. It will range from a simple or routine task to a complex or demanding task.

"So, here is our completed graph.

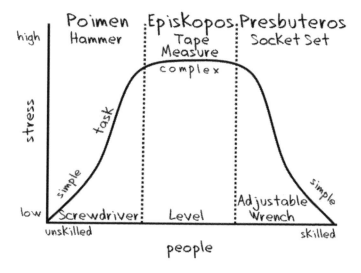

Christopher pulled up to Bob's house as Bob continued. "Tomorrow morning we will start looking more closely at each of the six leadership styles. Start thinking about what each of them would look like in the workplace. Thanks for the ride." With that, Bob retrieved his luggage and headed up to his house.

Christopher thought about what Bob said. *What would each of these look like in the workplace? More importantly*, he thought, *which is the right one to use in the workplace?* He thought about that question on his drive home.

THE DEFINITIONS

When Christopher got to the restaurant, he noticed Bob already inside. They greeted each other and Bob said, "We've got a lot to cover this morning, so I thought we should get right to it. I took the liberty of ordering for you."

Christopher thanked him and joked, "Have we been together so long that you've come to know what I like for breakfast?"

Bob laughed as he took a sip from his coffee. Then he got right to business. "So, without checking your notes, what are the drawers in your toolbox?"

"They are based on three Greek words in the Bible that are used to describe a leader. They are *poimen*, *presbuteros*, and *episkopos*," Christopher then joked, "I will take leadership styles for $200, Alex."

Christopher continued in his best Jeopardy portrayal, "What are two leadership styles contained in each of the drawers in your toolbox, for a total of six leadership styles?"

"And what are those leadership styles?" asked Bob.

"They are **Screwdriver**, **Hammer**, **Adjustable Wrench**, **Socket Set**, **Level** and **Measuring Tape!**" Christopher said with pride.

"And the last question for review, what are the leadership tasks that define the leadership styles?"

Christopher replied almost before the question left Bob's lips, "L.V.D.P.D. That is Listens, Visions, Delegates, Praises and Disciples."

"I'm not sure 'Visions' is a verb," quipped Bob.

"Okay, I like L.P.D.P.D. better anyway. Which is **Listens**, **Plans**, **Delegates**, **Praises** and **Disciples**," Christopher said sharply.

Bob looked proudly at Christopher like he had just scored his first touchdown. "Well done. The force is very strong with this one. Now let's get to my favorite part.

"So a leader listens to others in order to diagnose and solve problems, then he, as you said, 'visions' or plans by setting goals[31] and developing short- and long-term plans. When the plan is in place, he or she delegates to others the tasks to perform. Based on the

---

[31] John Cheydleur, "The Idea Behind Motivation," *Leadership* 1 (Summer 1980)   57-62.

monitoring[32] of the job, the leader will praise those performing the tasks by providing feedback and rewards. It is important also to disciple others by training people to do their job better. These are some of the skills or competencies that are necessary for a leader to be effective. Now, let's define our leadership styles in terms of these skills."

"Are we going to go deeper into how to perform these competencies?" Christopher asked. "It seems like they need practice in order to actually perform them."

"That is true," replied Bob, "but that is for another time. Maybe section two of your training.

The Poimen Drawer

"I will start with the first one, since I am probably more familiar with the Screwdriver leadership style. Then I will give you a chance to define the Hammer leadership style.

"Remember, a person with the *poimen* drive puts the task first. In a low-stress scenario, this person operates in the Screwdriver leadership style. A leader using the Screwdriver style does tasks themselves. Only one person can hold a screwdriver at a time and that screwdriver has one focused purpose, which is to drive screws. Leaders using this style will expect others they work with to be self-directed. If the work group is performing tasks that

---

[32]   Charles A. Van Wagner, "Supervision of Lay Pastoral Care," *Journal of Pastoral Care* 31 (March 1977): 158-63.

require little skill or expertise, they will expect others to simply perform without a lot of input.

"Leaders using the Screwdriver leadership style expect people to know their jobs and do them well. Therefore, they are likely to hear, but not listen. When it comes to communicating vision, they set goals[33] and plan more by example than actually sharing information.

> **The poimen drawer contains the Hammer and the Screwdriver Leadership Styles**

"That means they do not delegate directly; rather, they set the example that they expect others to follow. They take personal responsibility for success and failure. It makes it difficult for them to delegate because they feel no one can do the task as well as they can. Because of this, they will work tirelessly to try to accomplish tasks alone.

"They will give some praise related to task performance and they will reward good performance. They disciple and train others only if they emulate similar tendencies. They also tend to switch into the Hammer style when things go wrong.

"Now you take the next one."

"Wow, that is a tough act to follow, but what you don't know is that I have been studying. I've been doing some work around the house so I could

---

[33] David C. McClelland, "Goal Setting and Success," *Harvard Business Review*, June 1966, p. 127.

become more familiar with my tools and finish Danielle's honey-do list.

"Under high stress, a person with *poimen* drive operates in Hammer style. A Hammer expects compliance with their plans and instructions. After all, he or she is used to pounding nails, and I've learned through practice that nails will only go the direction you force them.

"Therefore, leaders in Hammer style do not emphasize listening to others. They dismiss the ideas or suggestions others have and are probably seen as unresponsive by their subordinates.

"Hammers do not cast vision and they develop only short-range goals and plans. They plan where the next nail goes or decide what nail didn't go in straight and needs pulled.

"They delegate with clear direction and expect instructions to be carried out by others. They don't take any back talk from the nails. Praise and rewards are rare. Their feedback tends to be negative and specific, just like when you hit your thumb.

"Hammers do not disciple or train others. Little hammers just have to learn by watching and doing what they are told. When the only tool you have is a hammer, everyone looks like a nail."

Bob said with a big smile, "Very good. Before long you'll be discipling someone else. ""Do you want to take the next one too?"

I wonder what he meant by discipling someone else, Christopher thought. "That's okay; I'll let you take it. That is really the only one I was prepared to do."

The Presbuteros Drawer

"No problem." Bob continued explaining, "Remember it's all about putting people first as opposed to putting the task first, as with the previous. In a low-stress situation, *presbuteros*-driven people operate with the Adjustable Wrench leadership style. Leaders in the Adjustable Wrench style put people first.[34]

"They listen a lot and are more interested in personal than task information. They do not cast vision or set goals. Neither do they make explicit plans other than for personal improvement. They prefer to adjust to the current status or scenario.

> **The presbuteros drawer contains the Socket Set and the Adjustable Wrench Leadership Styles**

"Adjustable Wrenches do not delegate clearly. They prefer to be flexible depending on the people involved and their needs. However, they encourage others to take action to improve themselves. They praise personal accomplishments and reward personal improvement, not task performance. Adjustable Wrenches will disciple others in personal areas;[35] however, they do not perform task related training.

---

[34]   Michael Youssef, *The Leadership Style of Jesus* (Wheaton, Illinois: Victor Books, 1986), p.50.

[35]   George Johnston, "Soul Care in the Ministry of Jesus," *Canadian Journal of Theology* 6 (1960): 25-30.

"So, under high stress, *presbuteros*-driven leaders operate in the Socket Set leadership style.[36] Leaders operating in the Socket Set style encourage participation; they want to get all the sockets in the group connected. They encourage people to participate in meetings while they listen to understand. After all, it's really the socket that drives the task. The ratchet is just there to provide leverage.

"Rather than cast vision, Socket Sets think that decisions should be made by consensus and that others should make plans. You have to find the right size that fits. You don't want to be using a 9/16" socket when what you really need is 14 mm. They do not delegate directly, but they try to match people and jobs—the right size for the task. They prefer to get consensus on direction.

"Socket Sets consider rewarding adequate or desirable performance as a good source of leverage and think of negative feedback as useful only in limited situations. They disciple others to develop skills, but only somewhat."

In the Episkopos Drawer

"Let's continue," Bob said. "When under low stress, a person with *episkopos* drive operates in the Bubble Level leadership style. Remember *episkopos* drive means mission first. Leaders operating in the Level style will guide subordinates toward high standards and improved performance. They want to make sure that everyone is lined out correctly.

---

[36] Youssef, *The Leadership Style of Jesus*, pp. 27-36.

"They definitely listen to understand. They are concerned about the organization's vision and high performance standards, but they feel that subordinates should focus on self-improvement and individualized goals. They are concerned about the subordinate's part in organization goals or plans.

"Levels are less directive when delegating, because they see their role as one of aiding or guiding others in their own performance. They ask others to develop plans, solutions to problems and alternate ways of accomplishing tasks as they simply guide for the best output. They also tend to minimize the focus on their own ideas and desire to be an aid to others in performing the task.

> **The episkopos drawer contains the Tape Measure and the Bubble Level leadership styles**

"Levels praise by providing frequent, specific, task-oriented feedback, [37] assistance and resources to help others improve. If a subordinate is a little off, they are quick to point out that they are 'off bubble.' They reward task performance and improvement of performance. Of course, by the very nature of a level, they make fine adjustments to keep people on track and therefore disciple others very effectively.

"Now, in high-stress situations, a leader with *episkopos* drive will operate in the Measuring Tape

---

[37] Alvin Jackson, "Honesty and Honor," *Leadership* 14 (Summer 1993): 68-69.

leadership style. Leaders in Measuring Tape style lead and make decisions.[38] They will measure twice and cut once.

"A Measuring Tape will solicit input from others on problems and decisions, but they leave no doubt about who makes the final decision. They might measure the situation from various angles, but when all is said and done, they decide the best-measured approach. They cast a clear vision[39] and set goals.[40] Measuring Tapes can stretch to reach both short- and long-range plans.

"They delegate in a clear and concise manner, but they are nice about it. However, they leave no doubt about what is expected. They can be concise to within 1/16 of an inch.

"Measuring Tapes will praise and reward fairly and firmly. They inform others of inadequate performance if a problem occurs, and you will always know if you measure up. They will communicate why improved performance is necessary.

"A leader in Measuring Tape Leadership Style will not directly disciple others, but he will delegate the responsibility for discipleship and training to others."

---

[38] LeRoy Lawson, "Firm and Fair," *Leadership* 14 (Summer 1993): 70-72.

[39] Dennis Sawyer, "Rekindling Vision in an Established Church," *Leadership* 14 (Summer 1993): 91.

[40] Craig B. Larson, "Handing Your Baby to Barbarians," *Leadership* 14 (Summer 1993): 47.

Christopher joked, "Sounds like the old Measuring Tape style is what our company is looking for in a leader; except for that 'nice about it' part." "Now, I know what you're going to say: 'It' 'depends on the amount of stress, the type of tasks and the people involved," he said in his best Bob imitation.

"You are correct, but you still have much to learn young grasshopper," Bob replied in his Master Po voice.

"Grasshopper? Huh?" Christopher said as he feigned confusion. *Great Kung Fu reference*, he thought. *Boy I really like this guy!*

"Never mind, it was before your time."

Christopher couldn't wait any longer; the suspense was eating at him. "Alright, I understand the definitions of each leadership style, but which one is the best?"

"The best?" Bob replied, sounding incredulous. "It depends... I gotta get to the office. We'll talk about it tomorrow."

THE BEST LEADERSHIP STYLE

When Christopher got home from work, he couldn't wait to share the definitions with Danielle. She pretended to be interested at first, but then she started to grasp what it all meant.

"So," she said, "Bob has given you a formula on how to lead? It sounds to me like all you have to do is switch to the right style for the stress level, the type of task and the skill level of the people you are leading."

"I know, but doesn't that sound too easy? If it were really that easy, I would never have had a bad boss or a horrible supervisor. There has to be a trick to it. I guess I will have to wait until breakfast to find out."

Then she asked, "What about people who are unmotivated? Where do they fit on the scale?"

"That's a very good question; let me channel Bob and see how he would answer that." He thought for half a minute, and then said, "You know I think he would say that the bottom axis could be a motivation level instead of a skill level. I remember him saying that skill fits our work place. Everyone we work with is motivated to work, otherwise they 'wouldn't stick around. Yes, that's what Bob would say."

Christopher looked as if he had something more to say, but then decided to keep it to himself.

Danielle, recognizing his look, asked, "What?"

"What, what?" he replied like always.

"You know; you have that look."

"What look?"

"That look that says, 'I have something I want to ask, but I already know the answer,'" She pressed, "What is it?"

He answered with a phony casualness, "Oh, it's just that Bob asked if we wanted to go with them to their church this weekend. The pastor that taught him some of this stuff is speaking. I kind of want to go, but I know you have made plans..."

Danielle interrupted, trying not to act too excited, "I'd love too. I can do my thing next weekend or maybe even during the week. Rose and I have been wanting to go out to that new Mexican restaurant, so you boys can take us out to dinner after church." She was still in shock that Christopher wanted to go to church. He had never in their eight years of marriage even uttered the word 'church'—that is, not until he met Bob.

By the time they went to bed, Christopher was able to occupy his mind with things other than leadership styles, drives and so forth. He really did have a big list of things to fix around the new house. After a long hard day, he once again slept through the night and woke to his alarm clock.

He arrived at the restaurant a few minutes early. As he walked in, he noticed Bob was not in their normal booth. Someone else had taken their spot. He considered switching into the Hammer leadership style and "nail" them, but thought better of it.

"I don't know if I can handle this change. Just too drastic," Christopher opened.

"I know what you mean. I hope the food doesn't taste any different from this angle," with a serious look on his face, Bob said, "Now, you had a question when we left yesterday?"

"Of course, which leadership style is best?"

"And I said, that depends." Bob continued, "Don't you remember Stress, Task and People—S.T.P.?"

"Sure, but there has to be one that is better than the rest." Christopher went on to say, "I can't imagine when I would use the Hammer leadership style, or what about the Socket Set leadership style? There would have to be very few times a leader would use it."

Bob thought to himself for a moment, and then asked, "Okay, then when do you think the Hammer leadership style would be effective?"

"Never. I can't think of a single time I would use the Hammer leadership style," Christopher answered honestly.

"Have you ever been in a life-and-death situation?" Bob asked very seriously.

"Not really."

Bob took a long sip of his coffee, and then he settled in to tell a story. Christopher recognized this look and he knew he was going to learn something important.

"There was this guy I knew named Rick. He was a retired army officer and he pretty much acted like one. Rick was a security specialist and because of that he thought everyone else should be as security-conscious as he was.

"Therefore, I witnessed Rick many times in the Hammer style of leadership. He always wanted us to practice for an emergency. He didn't understand we had real work to do. We joked about it, but Rick would come down hard on us.

"I eventually switched jobs and I lost track of Rick, but I knew he became the director of security for Morgan Stanley in New York. I read stories that Rick instituted some major changes while working for Morgan Stanley. He made stockbrokers and administrative assistants crawl out of their offices on their hands and knees. He didn't stop and take their opinions, and he didn't listen to their inputs—he just made them practice.

"Rick tried to get his company to move out of the World Trade Center, but he was unsuccessful. On September 11, 2001, Rick's planning and practice paid off. Rick's coworkers remembered all the drills Rick had put them through.

"Because of Rick's choice of leadership style, many lives were saved. Immediately after the first hijacked plane struck one World Trade Center, he ordered the company's 3800 employees to evacuate from World Trade Center buildings two and five. It took them just 45 minutes to get out to safety. Only 13 Morgan Stanley employees died that day; Rick and his security team died rescuing others who worked for companies that were not prepared."

Bob sat quietly eating his food. Christopher, a little choked up, knew better than to speak right now. He concentrated on finishing his breakfast.

After enough time had passed, Christopher said, "I understand. One specific time the Hammer leadership style is effective would be in a crisis or an emergency requiring a quick response—when there is no time for the leader to listen to ideas or take input from subordinates.

"Then it would also be effective when the leader has information or perspective the subordinates don't have. Like when an organization does not require subordinates to know everything the leaders know."

Bob joined in after finishing his last bite of eggs. "It is also effective when specific procedures must be followed exactly. For example, when minor deviations from procedure will result in serious problems.

"So then, when is the Hammer leadership style ineffective?"

Christopher had already thought through this, so he answered, "In situations like I am used to working in, where subordinates are expected to solve problems, take initiative or to innovate.

"Also, I would think it would be ineffective where I transferred from because special procedures were required due to our complex tasks."

"Good examples," Bob said, "What about the Measuring Tape leadership style? When would it be effective?"

"I just realized at this moment, that it would be effective where I just transferred from for the same reason the Hammer would not be—because special procedures were required due to our complex tasks.

"With the mix of experienced and rookie engineers working there, soliciting input from subordinates and communicating results of a decision and rationale were very important.

"A whole lot of decisions had to be made, but we had a lot of new engineers who did not have a clue. The engineers running the division, who had a comprehensive perspective, needed to make the appropriate decisions.

"I'm not really sure when the Measuring Tape would be ineffective. It seems to me that this one must be the best," finished Christopher.

Bob countered with, "I'm afraid you have missed one vital point. That is, there is no one best leadership style. They all can be effective, depending on the stress level in the scenario, the complexity of the task and the skill level of the people.

"On the other hand, any of the leader styles[41] can be ineffective in the wrong scenario. For example, the Measuring Tape leadership style can be ineffective when the leader does not have a more

---

[41] Beth E. Brown, "Practices of Leadership in the Context of Church," *Christian Educational Journal* 12 (January 1991): 107-14.

comprehensive perspective on the problem or issue than those working on it.

"Or when the status distinction between the leader and the subordinates is minimal. The Measuring Tape style is unnecessary when the leader is not required to make many decisions to facilitate effective completion of the task at hand. I'm sure now you can think of times when the Measuring Tape would not be the most effective style of leadership."

"Yes, I see your point. There is still not one magic bullet or secret leadership style that works in all scenarios," Christopher realized. "It takes all of them to be the most effective.

"I can see the Socket Set leadership style being effective at times when the Measuring Tape is not. Like when all subordinates are excellent performers and well suited to their jobs.

"Or at times when subordinates have as much information relevant to decisions and activities as does the leader. I have worked in situations where the Socket Set style was effective because the work activities needed to be conducted by people with a great deal of autonomy, but had to be coordinated among all those working on the project."

"Very good application," Bob said. He then added, "The Socket Set style could be just as ineffective when the manager has access to information or a perspective that the workers can't have. Then back to our original discussion, the Socket Set would not be effective in a crisis or when an emergency occurs that requires quick responses or decisions.

"The Socket Set style would also be ineffective if the people performing the task did not have an in-depth understanding of the work they are engaged in. Also, when workers must complete separate parts of a task, which, when combined, achieve the task goal.

"Do you want to keep going?" Bob asked

"Sure, we are on a roll and I am keeping up in my notebook."

"Great," Bob replied, "Then you take the Screwdriver style. When would it be effective and when would it be ineffective?"

Christopher nodded and then started. "The Screwdriver style is effective in situations where status distinctions between the leader and subordinates are small and possibly when performance goals and standards are clear to everyone working on the task.

"It is likely to be effective when workers must conduct their work independent of the leader, and when there is little coordination or integration among those on the project.

"Let me think about when it would be ineffective. What about at times when subordinates must perform the majority of the tasks?"

"Why would the Screwdriver leadership style be ineffective then?" asked Bob.

"Well, because the Screwdriver prefers to do the work and has trouble letting go or delegating.

"He also would be less than effective when coordination or integration is essential to the task. He probably doesn't work well when there are performance problems with one or more subordinates or when others must be discipled or trained by the leader."

"Sounds good," said Bob as he looked at his watch. "We better finish up. Let me take the Level leadership style.

"Level is an effective leadership style when working with moderately skilled people who have a desire to improve and when working in a low-stress scenario that allows for discipling and developing of subordinates.

"The Level is most effective when timely performance feedback is needed to improve performance. If the task is more complex, there would need to be enough time available to train those with lower skills and abilities.

"This style would be effective when working with a team[42] so that the organizational goals can be met even if one or more of the members do not meet their individual performance goals.

"The Level style is ineffective when the workers on the task are already skilled and able to make their own decisions. It could also be less effective in situations when decisions have to be made quickly to move forward.

"Levels could also be less than effective when the organization's performance is dependent on the attainment of performance goals by every one of the team.

---

[42] Howard Clark, "Time for Team Building," *Leadership* 14 (Summer 1993): 73-75.

"Of course the Level leadership style would not be effective in a crisis or emergency, unless it was practice for the real thing.

"Okay, we have time do go through the last one. Do you have any questions up to this point?" Bob asked.

"Nope. Let's look at the Adjustable Wrench leadership style. Do you mind if I take a stab at it?" asked Christopher. "I think it would be effective when tasks are routine."

"Routine? How so?" Bob asked.

"Like in a place where everyone knows what's to be done and how to do it—when performance is at an adequate or high level or in a situation when it's important that the leader and subordinates be friends and have a close relationship."

"Good analysis, I'm not sure I would have come up with that. I thought you would have focused on a vocational counselor as opposed to a leader functioning that way." Then Bob complimented Christopher saying, "I think you are ready to lead!"

"Before you kick me out of the nest, let me tell you where I think the Adjustable Wrench leadership style is ineffective.

"I don't think the Adjustable Wrench leadership style would work when tasks are unique or complex. It's definitely not effective when workers are not skilled or not motivated to take initiative or be innovative.

"The Adjustable Wrench would also not perform well when the leader is required to make decisions and only they have all of the information or perspective needed to make those decisions."

"You are ready to fly the coop and be out on your own," Bob joked. "But before you go, let me share some points to consider when interpreting and applying different leadership styles.

"There is no style which is effective all of the time. Everyone has a preferred style of leadership that he or she uses most frequently. Some people have back-up styles, which they use in situations requiring a style other than their most preferred. People can also vary in which back-up style they use according to the demands of the particular scenario.

"Leaders are often surprised to find they have seemingly opposing dominant and back-up leadership styles. One example is very common, the combination of Measuring Tape and Socket Set. Upon reflection they usually recognize that they use one style with one type of person or situation. They might use the Socket Set style when dealing with individuals who know their jobs and are highly skilled, then use a Measuring Tape style with less-skilled workers or when things start to go wrong.

"Remember the code in the Bible uses all of these words to describe one person. Specifically it describes the leader of the church. Therefore, it should not surprise us that a combination of several is the most effective.

"I am going to give you a Leadership Style Evaluation. This will help you decipher your personal leadership style. It will tell you what your preferred styles are.

"Now hear this, Christopher: don't fall into the trap of placing either a positive or negative value on any of the labels used to describe these styles. Don't assume that a particular style is effective in your new job until you learn all the aspects of the job. You can't evaluate it until you know all of the specific tasks and until you determine the characteristics of your people.

"Also, you need to realize there is a need to change styles over time. 'Life-cycle' theories of leadership suggest that different leadership styles are appropriate at different stages in an individual's or work group's progress toward the ability to work effectively together or alone. Theoretically, as divisions, departments, work groups or individual members mature, people move away from a relatively unknowledgeable, passive-dependent position requiring firm leadership direction. Many will start with the Hammer or Measuring Tape leadership style. Then the group will develop to a point where they know their jobs and are independently driven or motivated,[43] where they are best lead through participation and delegation, as in the Level or Socket Set leadership style."

---

[43] John Cheydleur, "The Idea Behind Motivation," *Leadership* 1 (Summer 1980): 58.

EPILOGUE

Christopher and Bob continued to meet one or two mornings each week for breakfast. Bob's wife, Rose, and Christopher's wife, Danielle, became close friends, which was not always good for the guys. It turned out they both liked flea markets, so each of the guys would come home to find new bargains decorating their house.

At work, Christopher was turning into a top-notch leader. He was learning the competencies and skills necessary to be effective. Those skills, along with his recently acquired knowledge of leadership styles and drives, made him the go-to guy when there were challenges in the plant. Christopher became so skilled at managing meetings that actually accomplished something that people all over the company were trying to recruit him for their committees.

Christopher had learned from the leadership evaluation he took that his primary style of leading was the Screwdriver. This made sense to him after reviewing it with Bob. He had worked independently for so long that it was natural for him to feel comfortable in Screwdriver leadership style. He discovered the problem came when the stress level was turned up. He discovered, as Bob's graph predicted, that he moved into Hammer leadership style. However, the Hammer was not the appropriate style for his moderate- to highly-skilled subordinates. He now uses S.T.P. and makes conscious decisions how he will behave and what style he will use in a given scenario.

Christopher and Danielle went to church with Bob and Rose. It was so different from what they experienced growing up. This church was alive and fun. They found the messages weren't at all what they expected; they left every week with useful information that helped in different areas of their lives. Their marriage had never been better, they even learned how to get their debt under control and, of course, the leadership principles helped Christopher excel in his new position. Christopher even sold his leased car and bought a beater like Bob until he could pay off his debt.

The leadership principles Christopher learned were so valuable to him that he decided there might be other ideas that could be helpful in the Bible. He read through the entire New Testament. Bob advised him to start with the book of John, the fourth book in the New Testament.

One day at breakfast with Bob, Christopher asked, "I read one section of the Bible in the book about the Romans. It was chapter 10 verses— six through 10.

But the righteousness based on faith says, "Do not say in your heart, 'Who will ascend into heaven?'" (that is, to bring Christ down) "Or 'Who will descend into the abyss?'" (that is, to bring Christ up from the dead). But what does it say? "The word is near you, in your mouth and in your heart" (that is, the word of faith that we proclaim); because, if you confess with your mouth that Jesus is Lord and believe in your heart that God raised him from the dead, you will be saved. For with the heart one believes and is justified, and with the mouth one confesses and is saved.

"I really think that's something I need to do. I'm just not sure I completely understand what to do."

"What part do you have questions about?" asked Bob.

"That part in verse nine,

If you confess with your mouth that Jesus is Lord and believe in your heart that God raised him from the dead, you will be saved.

"Before, I didn't really believe this. But everything else I've checked out in the Bible appears to be true, so why would the part about Jesus be any different? If God got the leadership stuff right and the history part right, then why would He make a mistake about this salvation part? I'm just not a religious person."

Bob took in a deep breath. "Remember, when we first met, I told you that I was not religious either. Religion is about trying to earn something you don't deserve, but grace is God giving you something you don't deserve and can never earn. It is about having a relationship with God through His Son, Jesus.

"If you believe Jesus died in your place and paid the penalty for your sins, then by faith you accept that it is true and verse nine tells us, '**you will be saved**'. Notice it doesn't say 'could be saved' or 'might be saved,' but *will* be saved.

"And I think Romans 10:10 says it best,

For with the heart one believes and is justified, and with the mouth one confesses and is saved.

"So, are you telling me that you believe this to be true in your heart?"

Christopher looked thoughtfully at Bob and immediately said, "Absolutely."

"Then," Bob said, "what's stopping you from doing the last part that says, 'with the mouth one confesses and is saved'?"

"Nothing at all." Christopher started to pray, "Dear Jesus, I want to thank you for dying on the cross for my sins. I'm sorry it took me so long to believe that, but now I got it. Would you forgive me for my sins and save me? Amen."

And they lived happily ever after—actually that isn't quite true. There were many challenges ahead of them; leadership challenges and spiritual challenges. However, Christopher and Danielle, along with Bob and Rose, became lifetime friends. When they faced challenges; they faced them together.

THE TOOLS EXPLAINED
Part 2

THE HISTORY OF THE CODE

The basis for the Leader Code is three Greek words used in the New Testament of the Bible to describe a leader. These words are translated into English in a variety of ways, depending on the context. The Greek words are *poimen*, pronounced poy-mane, which means pastor or shepherd; *episkopos*, pronounced ep-is'-kop-os, which means bishop or overseer; and *presbuteros*, pronounced pres-boo'-ter-os, which means elder.

These three Greek words are translated to describe a leader in different situations. In English we use the words *pastor*, *bishop* and *elder* to describe the leader of the church. Some denominational churches will assign these titles to different leaders in their denomination. It is important to understand that the Bible does not give any commands pertaining to church government. A denomination is free to design its own form of church government based on these words; however, the use of these words in the first century was applied to the same individual as we see in the Bible. There are several passages that use two or three of these words in the same context to describe the same individual.

For example, we read from the apostle Peter, who was also an elder, admonishing the other elders in their work in1 Peter 5:1-3,

So I exhort the elders (*presbuteros*) among you, as a fellow elder and a witness of the sufferings of Christ, as well as a partaker in the glory that is going to be revealed: shepherd the flock (this is the verb form of the noun *poimen*) of God that is among you, exercising oversight (*episkopos*), not under compulsion, but willingly, as God would have you; not for shameful gain, but eagerly; not domineering over those in your charge, but being examples to the flock.

We learn that elders (*presbuteros*) are to serve as overseers by having oversight (*episkopos*) as they shepherd (the verb form of *poimen*) the flock. He is giving direction to the leaders to carry out the functions of a leader. He is exhorting them not to neglect one area or another. They are to take care of the work of the church as a pastor, minister to the people of the church as an elder and supervise the work of the church as the bishop.

While it is perfectly acceptable for denominational leaders to delegate one or more of those roles to different people, a leader cannot abdicate his or her responsibility to influence and manage people so that they accomplish the work to achieve the organization's mission.

The apostle Paul, who wrote the majority of the New Testament, knew his time of leading churches was going to end. So, he instructed one of his protégés on how to select church leaders in Titus 1:5-7,

This is why I left you in Crete, so that you might put what remained into order, and appoint elders (*presbuteros*) in every town as I directed you—if anyone is above reproach, the husband of one wife, and his children are believers and not open to the charge of debauchery or insubordination. For an overseer (*episkopos*), as God's steward, must be above reproach. He must not be arrogant or quick-tempered or a drunkard or violent or greedy for gain,

Notice that Paul instructs Titus to appoint elders. You did not just become an elder by virtue of being old enough. This was an appointed position or calling, responsible to oversee the church as a bishop, and in other passages they are instructed to lead the flock as a shepherd or pastor. For example, in Acts 20:17,

Now from Miletus he sent to Ephesus and called the elders (*presbuteros*) of the church to come to him.

and in Acts 20:28,

> **Pay careful attention to yourselves and to all the flock (derivative of *poimen*), in which the Holy Spirit has made you overseers (*episkopos*), to care for the church of God, which he obtained with his own blood.**

Each of these words describe a leader in the New Testament Church. There is a reason that God chose to use three different words with different meanings to describe this job of leading. Each of these words describes a different focus or function. Upon careful examination and evaluation, you will see that each one represents a different drive or motivation of an individual. We know from modern studies of drive, or motivation that one's drive will lead to related thoughts typical of that drive. The typical thoughts of these three drives will then cause expected behaviors that reflect the drive. These behaviors, when appropriate for the situation—the stress level, the complexity or simplicity of the task at hand and the skill and/or motivation level of the workers— determine the effectiveness of the leader.

By observing and classifying these behaviors, the dominant leadership style of the leader can be determined. The six leadership styles in prior research were classified as pastor, shepherd, counselor, elder, teacher and bishop. While these names were more descriptive of the leadership styles, they also lead to confusion with the offices in the church by the same name. The author has taught these principles in other countries that did not speak English and determined that these names also do not translate easily. For example, in Spanish, the word for pastor and shepherd is the same word. This lead to the adoption of the Screwdriver, Hammer, Adjustable Wrench, Socket Set, Bubble Level and Tape Measure as the titles for the six leadership styles.

Using the names of tools as titles for the leadership styles helped to create a vivid picture of how each style functions, making them more memorable. In addition to describing the leadership styles as tools, the inner drives that are indicative of the three Greek words can be described as drawers in a toolbox. This completes the imagery for the student leader. It helps make the abstract subject of situation leadership more concrete in the mind of the learner.

Therefore, the three Greek words are the origins of what we know of leadership. It is the leadership code that pulls it all together. These Greek words describe the inner drives or motivation that people have. The drives are represented as drawers that a leader can open to access leadership skills, abilities, styles and methods.

Each of these three drawers contains two leadership styles, for a total of six. Each leadership style is defined by how it does the following:

1. Listens to subordinates in order to diagnose and solve problems.
2. Casts vision by setting goals; develop long- and short-term plans.
3. Delegates and directs others to perform tasks.
4. Praises by providing feedback and rewards.
5. Disciples by training and developing others.

WHAT DRIVES US

The three Greek words *poimen, presbuteros* and *episkopos*, are the source of what we understand of leadership. These words describe the inner drives or motivation that people have. The *poimen* drive puts the **Task First.** The *presbuteros* drive puts **People First.** The *episkopos* drive puts the **Mission First.** The drives are represented as drawers that a leader can open to access leadership skills, abilities, styles and methods.

There are many theories about why human beings do what they do. Social scientists have been trying to explain human behavior since the beginning of the study of social science. It appears that we, as humans, act the way we do because of a drive that is deep inside of us. We each have an internal, intrinsic, unseen drive that results in behaviors that are extrinsic and observable.

The concept of intrinsic motivation emerged from the work of Harlow (1953) and White (1959) in opposition to the behavioral theories that were dominant at the time. Intrinsically motivated behaviors were defined as those that are not energized by physiological drives or their derivatives and for which the reward is the spontaneous satisfaction associated with the activity itself rather than with operationally separable consequences. Intrinsic motivation is the motivational instantiation of the proactive, growth-oriented nature of human beings. Indeed, it is intrinsically motivated activity that is the basis for people's learning and development. White suggested that a need for competence underlies intrinsic motivation—that people engage in many activities in order to experience a sense of effectiveness and joy. Later, deCharms (1968) proposed that people have a primary motivational propensity to engage in activities that allow them to feel a sense of personal causation and that this is the basis of intrinsic motivation. Thus, White and deCharms together were proposing that the needs for competence and autonomy are the energizing basis for intrinsically motivated behavior.[44]

As individuals, what motivates or drives us, as Daniel Pink puts it in his book *Drive: The Surprising*

---

[44] Edward L. Deci and Maarten Vansteenkiste, *Self-Determination Theory and Basic Need,* (University of Rochester, U.S.A. and University of Leuven, Belgium, 2004). p. 4

Truth about what Motivates Us[45], is intrinsic. That drive or motivation comes from within each person. Pink says, "That first drive (Motivation 1.0) didn't fully account for who we are. We also had a second drive—to seek rewards and avoid punishment more broadly.[46]

Pink goes on to say, "To help your employees find autonomy, the best strategy for an employer would be to figure out what's important to each individual employee.[47]" These are the three drives that Don referred to as drawers of a toolbox. They represent three areas that are important to most employees.

A great deal of the research into motivation and drive is summarized in these seven statements:

1. Leaders need to understand that normal, healthy adults have potential energy stored that we call *drive*.

2. Adults have access to this stored energy, and it manifests itself as these three drives.

3. Adults vary widely in how much of each drive they will have. Some will have more or less *poimen* drive than another person might have, and so on.

4. Whether one of the drives manifests itself into thoughts and behaviors or not depends on the specific situation in which the person finds him- or herself.

5. The specific circumstances of a situation can trigger a different drive. Each drive will manifest itself in response to a different set of circumstances.

---

[45] Daniel Pink, *Drive: The Surprising Truth about what Motivates Us,* (New York: Penguin Books, 2011).

[46] Ibid. p. 16.

[47] Ibid. p. 106.

6. Since the three drives are directed toward different kinds of goals, i.e. Task, People or Mission, the behavior that results from arousal of a drive is quite distinct for each one. In other words, each drive leads to a distinct pattern of behavior.

7. When the circumstances of a situation change, a different drive could be aroused, resulting in different patterns of behavior.

These intrinsic drives are the needs, or wants, that are related to our goals. What drives us determine our thoughts. Our thoughts impact our behaviors. Our behavior or our actions lead us to accomplish our goals.

DRIVE > THOUGHT > BEHAVIOR > GOAL ACCOMPLISHMENT

Another way to define our terms and understand how each interacts with the other is to examine the equation that Mitch offered as a manager's approach to understanding drive. A person's behavior is the product of their intrinsic drive and the circumstances of the situation.

$$B = D \times S$$
(BEHAVIOR = DRIVE x SITUATION)

Since D, or drive, is a constant, you can solve for B, or behavior, by observing how S, or the situation, has changed. Situations impact thoughts and concerns that will cause a person's behavior to change. For example, if a person goes to a party where there are many interesting and friendly people, he or she is likely to respond with *presbuteros* behaviors—people first. If a person works in a job or for a leader and receives no responsibility, opportunity to perform better or feedback on performance, this individual is unlikely to demonstrate *poimen* behaviors.

The first drive is *poimen*. This is the drive to achieve, to get the task completed. The *poimen* drive is an intrinsic drive to put the task first.

Thoughts of the *poimen* drive include, thinking about:

- Outperforming other people at work
- Meeting their self-imposed standards of excellence
- Offering unique contributions to a project
- Advancing one's career

These thoughts will lead to behaviors like:

- Setting goals for themselves
- Looking forward to getting feedback about how they are doing on the job
- Frequently taking initiative and being innovative
- Taking personal responsibility if things go wrong
- Spending time with experts over friends

The leaders who are driven by *poimen* drive are what John Maxwell, in his book *The 5 Levels of*

Leadership, calls level one leaders.[48] They rely upon their positional authority. People follow them because they have the position or title.

The second drive is *presbuteros.* This is the drive to be friendly, to be a people person. The *presbuteros* drive is an intrinsic drive to put people first.

Thoughts of the *presbuteros* drive include, thinking about:

- Developing close friendships
- Maintaining friendships in the workplace
- Spending time with others just to enjoy their company
- Desiring to restore relationships as soon as possible when they have been separated
- Seeing group activities as social occasions

These thoughts will lead to behaviors like:

- Having many friends
- Talking to or texting others frequently
- Using business email for personal correspondence
- Making a lot of phone calls
- Work-related calls or visits end up being more personal in nature
- Choosing to work with other people than be alone

---

[48] John C. Maxwell, *The 5 Levels of Leadership* (New York: Center Street, 2011). p. 7.

- Choosing friends to work with over experts
- Striving to gain personal approval from coworkers and supervisors
- Communicating in terms of how others think and feel
- Empathizing, sympathizing and consoling coworkers

Leaders who are driven by the *presbuteros* drive are what John Maxwell calls level two leaders.[49] They rely upon their relationships with their subordinates to lead. People follow them because they know, like and trust them.

The third drive is *episkopos*. This is the drive to influence people to accomplish the mission. The *episkopos* drive is an intrinsic drive to put the mission first.

Thoughts of the *episkopos* drive include, thinking about:

- Taking strong and forceful actions
- Giving help, advice, support - many times unsolicited
- Strategizing about how to influence people
- Directing or controlling a situation
- Considering the impact of their actions and how coworkers will feel or be influenced
- Maintaining status, reputation, and position

---

[49] Ibid. p. 8.

These thoughts will lead to behaviors like:

- Being active in organizational politics
- Frequently seeking positions of leadership
- Influencing people through control or persuasion, or offers of help or assistance
- Training subordinates and help them improve their task performance
- Seeking, withholding, using information to influence people
- Spending time with people who get things done

Leaders who are driven by the *episkopos* drive are what Maxwell calls level three leaders.[50] They have proven themselves by producing results and therefore people will follow them.

Maxwell explains that the five levels are like a building—all the higher levels rest on the lower ones.[51] He also explains that a leader must pass through every level to get to the next one. Level two builds on level one and, therefore, you cannot be a level three leader until you have mastered level two, which is permission. Once you have built a relationship with your people, you are ready to focus on producing results. Level three is the production level. This is where leadership really takes off and goes to another level.[52]

---

[50] Ibid.

[51] Ibid. p. 11.

[52] Ibid. p. 133.

Level three qualifies and separates true leaders from people who merely occupy leadership positions. Good leaders always make things happen. They get results. They accomplish the organization's mission. Just as *poimen* was task first and *presbuteros* was people first, leaders who are driven by *episkopos* put the mission first.

These leaders can make a significant impact on an organization. Not only are they productive individually, but because they are in charge, they are able to help the team produce. This ability gives leaders who are driven by *episkopos* confidence, credibility and increased influence. Maxwell says that no one can fake level three.[53] Either you are producing for the organization and getting something done or you are not.

---

[53] Ibid. p. 133-34.

THE BELL CURVE

The Blakeslee Theory of Leadership or "The Leader Code" is best represented on a graph. Dividing the graph into three somewhat equal sections, these sections represent the three intrinsic drives or motivations – drawers of the toolbox.

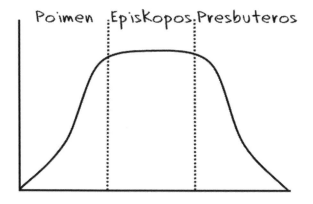

The graph with the three sections is overlaid on top of a bell curve. Then the six leadership styles – the tools – are added within each drawer. The drawers represent the drive or motivation that drives or supports that particular leadership style. See below.

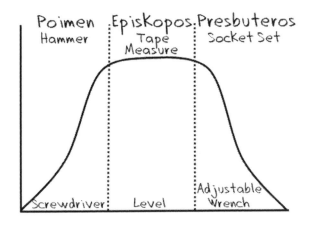

In each drawer you will find two leadership styles. The Hammer and Screwdriver leadership styles are driven by *poimen*. The Socket Set and the Adjustable Wrench leadership styles are driven by *presbuteros*. The Measuring Tape and the Bubble Level leadership styles are driven by *episkopos*.

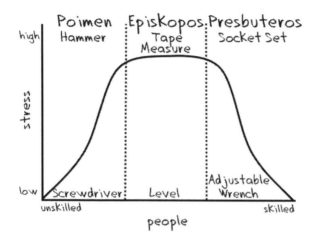

The next part of the graph is the X and Y-axes. The X-axis is PEOPLE and the Y-axis is STRESS. People range from unskilled to skilled, unmotivated to motivated, inflexible to flexible, out of shape to physically fit, etc. The X-axis can be changed to reflect how an organization might classify the workforce. Keep in mind; this is not set in stone. The goal is to make your work environment more effective.

This is not a hard science, like our friends in this story joked. It is important to realize that this graphical representation if far from absolute truth. It is a generalization of how this theory of leadership plays out in real life. There are no hard and fast rules for human behavior. Your subordinates may respond differently than expected to one or more leadership styles.

The bell curve is labeled for the type of task being performed. It may range from a simple or routine task to a complex or demanding task. Note that the bell curve is relatively flat on top and extends slightly into each section. This is partly because of the flaw in the idea of a bell curve representing tasks. There will be many times in an organization that your most skilled workers will be performing your most complex tasks. This flatter design was the solution for this dilemma.

When working with unskilled workers in a low-stress scenario, a leader could operate in the Screwdriver leadership style. With those same workers in a high-stress scenario or in an emergency, the leader may transition to a Hammer leadership style. However, if your workers are highly skilled, then using the Socket Set leadership style in high-stress situation could be more appropriate and shifting to the Adjustable Wrench style in low-stress situations with the same skilled people may be effective. If you have people who are moderately skilled, ideally you would use either the Bubble Level leadership style or Measuring Tape leadership style, depending on the level of stress in the situation.

LEADERSHIP STYLES

The Leader Code comes from three Greek words that have already been discussed extensively. These Greek words represent what drives most people. People who are driven by *poimen* put the **Task First.** People who are driven by *presbuteros* put **People First.** People who are driven by *episkopos* put the **Mission First**. We have already seen how these intrinsic drives are the needs, or wants, that are related to our goals.

Our drive determines our thoughts. Our thoughts impact our behaviors. Our behavior or our actions lead us to accomplish our goals. Our behaviors, or how we carry out our actions, indicates what style of leadership we are using. Leadership style can be a conscious decision or it can happen naturally based on what drives us, which in turn impacts our thoughts and then behaviors.

The three drives lead to behaviors which have been classified as six the leadership styles. There are two leadership styles associated with each of the drives. There is a high-stress *poimen* leadership style and a low-stress *poimen* leadership style. There is a high-stress *presbuteros* leadership style and a low-stress *presbuteros* leadership style. There is a high-stress *episkopos* leadership style and a low-stress *episkopos* leadership style.

To simplify the memorization and explanation of the leadership styles, each has been assigned a common tool that represents the behaviors of the leadership style. The *poimen* drive leads to the Hammer and Screwdriver leadership styles. Then the *presbuteros* drive leads to the Socket Set and the Adjustable Wrench leadership styles, while the *episkopos* drive leads to the Measuring Tape and the Bubble Level leadership styles

Each of these leadership styles can be described in terms of several behaviors that leaders display. These behaviors are actually the skills that every leader must have. Each of these skills impact subordinates in some way. How these skills are performed or executed is dependent on the behaviors associated with the drive that leads to the particular leadership style.

The skills are as follows:

1. Listens to subordinates in order to diagnose and solve problems
2. Casts vision by setting goals; develop long- and short-term plans
3. Delegates; directs others to perform tasks

4. Praises by providing feedback and rewards
5. Disciples by training and developing others

Poimen-Driven Leadership Styles

As previously stated, a person with the *poimen* drive will put the task first. In a low-stress scenario, they operate in the Screwdriver leadership style. Leaders using the Screwdriver style perform tasks themselves. Only one person can hold a screwdriver at a time and that screwdriver has one focused purpose: to drive screws. Leaders using this style will expect others they work with to be self-directed. If the work group is performing tasks that require little skill or expertise, they will expect others to simply perform without a lot of input.

Screwdriver Leaders:

1. Expect people to know their jobs and do them well (probably hear, but do not listen).
2. Communicate vision and goals, and plan by example.
3. Do not delegate directly; rather, they set the example, take personal responsibility for success and failure and, because they find it difficult to delegate, work, unceasingly to try to accomplish tasks alone.
4. Give some praise related to task performance and reward good performance.
5. Disciples and train subordinates only to the extent that they model him or her.

These leaders tend to switch into the Hammer style when things go wrong. This transition can occur without any outward indication. There is a certain stress level that when reached pushes a Screwdriver leader across the line to the Hammer style. Under high stress, a person with *poimen* drive operates in Hammer leadership style.

A Hammer expects compliance with their plans and instructions. After all, he or she is used to pounding nails and nails will only go in the direction you force them.

Hammer Leaders:

1. Do not emphasize listening to others' ideas or suggestions; may be seen as unresponsive to subordinates.

2. Do not cast vision and develop only short-range goals and plans.

3. Delegate with clear directions and expect their plans and instructions to be carried out by others.

4. Praise and reward rarely and give feedback that tends to be negative and specific.

5. Do not disciple or train others but expect them to know their jobs or simply do what they are told.

When the only tool you have is a hammer, everyone looks like a nail.

Presbuteros Driven Leadership Styles

A person with *presbuteros* drive will put people first.[54] In a low-stress situation, the *presbuteros* drive operates in the Adjustable Wrench leadership style.

Adjustable Wrench Leaders:

1. Listen a lot and are more interested in personal than task information.
2. Do not cast vision and/or set goals standards, and do not make explicit plans other than for personal improvement.
3. Do not delegate clearly, but encourage others to determine take action.
4. Praise personal accomplishments and reward personal improvement, not task performance.
5. Disciple others in personal areas[55]; do not perform task-related training.

Under high stress, a person with *presbuteros* drive operates in the Socket Set leadership style.[56] Leaders operating in the Socket Set style encourage participation.

---

[54] Michael Youssef, *The Leadership Style of Jesus* (Wheaton, Illinois: Victor Books, 1986), p.50.
[55] George Johnston, "Soul Care in the Ministry of Jesus," *Canadian Journal of Theology* 6 (1960): 25-30.
[56] Youssef, *The Leadership Style of Jesus*, pp. 27-36.

Socket Set Leaders:

1. Encourage people to participate in meetings while they listen to understand.
2. Rather than cast vision, think that decisions should be made by consensus and that the others should make plans.
3. Do not delegate directly, and try to match people and jobs and get consensus on direction.
4. Consider rewarding adequate or desirable performance as a motivator and think of negative feedback as useful only in very limited situations.
5. Disciple others to develop skills, but only somewhat.

Episkopos-Driven Leadership Styles

Under low stress, a person with *episkopos* drive operates in the Bubble Level leadership style. *Episkopos* drive means mission first. Leaders operating in the Level style guide subordinates toward high standards and improved performance. They also tend to minimize the focus on their own ideas.

Bubble Level leaders

1. Listen to understand.
2. Are not concerned about vision or high performance standards, but feel that subordinates should focus on self-improvement and individualized goals, not on the organization goals or plans.

3. Are less directive when delegating and see their role as one of aiding or guiding others in their own performance toward high standards; they ask others to develop plans, create solutions to problems and come up with alternate ways of accomplishing tasks and minimize the focus on their ideas;

4. Praise by providing frequent, specific, task-oriented feedback,[57] assistance and resources to help others improve; reward task performance and improvement of performance.

5. Disciple others very effectively.

In high-stress situations, a leader with *episkopos* drive will operate in the Measuring Tape leadership style. Leaders in Measuring Tape style lead and make decisions.[58] They will measure twice and cut once.

Measuring Tape leaders:

1. Solicit input from others on problems and decisions, but leave no doubt about who makes the final decision.

2. Cast clear visions and set goals; develop both short- and long-range plans.

3. Delegate clearly and concisely and are nice about it, but leave no doubt about what is expected.

---

[57] Alvin Jackson, "Honesty and Honor," *Leadership* 14 (Summer 1993): 68-69.

[58] LeRoy Lawson, "Firm and Fair," *Leadership* 14 (Summer 1993): 70-72.

4. Praise and reward firmly and fairly; inform others of inadequate performance if a problem occurs and communicate the rationale for needing improved performance;

5. Do not directly disciple others, but delegate the responsibility for discipleship and training to others.

LEADERSHIP SKILLS

Each of the six leadership styles can be described in terms of several behaviors that leaders display. These behaviors, when performed effectively, are the skills necessary for proper leadership. Each of these skills impact subordinates in some way. How these skills are performed is dependent on the drive that leads to the particular leadership style.

This is not meant to be an all-inclusive list of skills necessary for effective leadership. These are only those that have been selected as a measure to determine the leadership style being displayed.

The skills are as follows:

1. Listens to subordinates in order to diagnose and solve problems
2. Casts vision by setting goals; develop long- and short-term plans
3. Delegates; directs others to perform tasks

4. Praises by providing feedback and rewards
5. Disciples by training and developing others

The following is a more detailed discussion of the behaviors examined to determine the effectiveness of an individual's leadership style. Suggestions are made for proper evaluation and use of the skills listed.

1. Listens to subordinates in order to diagnose and solve problems

Do you really know how to listen or do you just know how to hear? If a leader needs to diagnose and solve problems, then they must be able to do more than hear what is being said—they must be able to listen to the person.

Listening involves understanding the situation from a perspective of another person. It is the ability to diagnose the situation with evidence to back up the conclusion. Listening allows the leader to responds to people appropriately in order to get the job done.

Don read from James 1:19 and told Mitch that we need to be quick to hear and slow to anger. If you were to examine this passage in the context, it is telling us to listen to God and act on what He says. James 1:19-21 tells us to listen and do what He says, without becoming angry. This principle can be translated into the work place. You may not hear what you want to hear, but you need to listen and act on the information given.

There are some behaviors that the leader will use to demonstrate active listening.

The leader will:

• Make eye contact with the speaker, nodding in agreement when appropriate
• Repeat back statements made by the speaker
• Paraphrase to the speaker what was said in their own words
• Ask for clarification to make sure the message was received properly

Remember the goal in listening is not agreement; it is understanding.

2. Casts vision by setting goals; develop long- and short-term plans

There has been much written and discussed recently on goal setting, and some of it is good. We all know that it helps make us more efficient and effective, but that does not mean that we actually do it. One of the more popular methods of goal setting, in recent years, is the SMART method. [59] This method of goal setting is in common use and is usually attributed to Peter Drucker and his teachings on "Management by Objectives" first released in his 1954 book *The Practice of Management.*

---

[59] G. T. Doran, "There's a S.M.A.R.T. way to write management's goals and objectives." *Management Review* (AMA FORUM, 1981) 70 (11): pp. 35–36.

I believe the idea of setting SMART goals goes back a further than that. I believe Jesus explained the need in Luke 14:28-31,

For which of you, desiring to build a tower, does not first sit down and count the cost, whether he has enough to complete it? Otherwise, when he has laid a foundation and is not able to finish, all who see it begin to mock him, saying, "This man began to build and was not able to finish." Or what king, going out to encounter another king in war, will not sit down first and deliberate whether he is able with ten thousand to meet him who comes against him with twenty thousand?

SMART is an acrostic for writing proper goals:

1. Specific—A SMART goal identifies a specific action or event that will take place.

2. Measurable—The description of a SMART goal will allow you to determine your progress towards completion and let you know when you are finished

3. Achievable—A SMART goal should be achievable given available resources.

4. Realistic—A SMART goal should require you to stretch beyond your normal routine and regular abilities, but allow for likely success based on your skills and the time available.

5. Time-Based—A SMART goal should state the specific time period in which it will be accomplished.

Different variations on this model have been used over the years. Some assign the letter A to Assignable, Appropriate, Actionable, Aligned, etc.

There are some behaviors that a leader will use to demonstrate when setting goals and planning.

The leader will:
- Set goals and performance standards
- Establish specific work goals
- Be concerned with performance standards
- Revise goals to make them realistic
- Set deadlines for task accomplishment
- Identify action steps, resources or obstacles involved in reaching an objective
- Prepare a schedule and set priorities

3. Delegates; directs others to perform tasks

Delegation is very important but more specifically, it's about how one delegates. In Exodus 18:17-23 Moses' father-in-law gave him some clear advice about delegation. He told Moses..

Moses' father-in-law said to him, "What you are doing is not good. You and the people with you will certainly wear yourselves out, for the thing is too heavy for you. You are not able to do it alone. Now obey my voice; I will give you advice, and God be with you! You shall represent the people before God and bring their cases to God, and you shall warn them about the statutes and the laws, and make them know the way in which they must walk and what they must do. Moreover, look for able men from all

the people, men who fear God, who are trustworthy and hate a bribe, and place such men over the people as chiefs of thousands, of hundreds, of fifties, and of tens. And let them judge the people at all times. Every great matter they shall bring to you, but any small matter they shall decide themselves. So it will be easier for you, and they will bear the burden with you. If you do this, God will direct you, you will be able to endure, and all this people also will go to their place in peace.

Jethro advised Moses to setup a chain of command so he would not burn out from doing all the work himself. I've known many leaders along the way that could have benefited from this small piece of advice.

Delegation is similar to setting goals. The difference is that you are assigning responsibility for completion to someone else. However, the same methods can be employed, including the SMART method.

There are some behaviors that a leader will use to demonstrate when delegating.

The leader will:

• Clearly assign authority and responsibility for task accomplishment to others
• Use the chain of command to get subordinates to share in task management
• Encourage others to seek task management responsibility by methods other than by ordering them to perform a task

Effective delegation is critical to achieving goals and successful leadership. The effective leader is able to set priorities, schedule tasks and assign work to others in a way that motivates them by giving them increased opportunity for achievement and control over their work. Under ideal circumstances, effective delegation begins with involving subordinates in the development of work goals and plans. Usually, however, the leader ends up working alone or with his or her supervisor to develop these goals and plans. The process of delegation will then begin after the planning is over. It starts by communicating the task assignments to subordinates. Clear communication and increased motivation are the marks of effective delegation no matter what the circumstances.

Two Keys to Effective Delegation

1. The clearer the understanding a subordinate has of what is to be accomplished, the greater the chances of accomplishing it.

2. The greater the sense of accomplishment a subordinate derives from doing a task, the greater his or her drive to complete the task.

4. Praises by providing feedback and rewards

After delegation, it is important for a leader to praise his or her people. This simply involves giving feedback about the tasks that were delegated and rewarding people for doing a good job.[60] In a classic leadership book, *The One Minute Manager*, Kenneth Blanchard says, "Help people reach their full potential, catch them doing something right."[61]

It also means providing negative feedback when the job was not performed as expected. The apostle Paul wrote a couple of letters to the church in Corinth giving them negative feedback about their performance. He said in 2 Corinthians 7: 8,

For even if I made you grieve with my letter, I do not regret it—though I did regret it, for I see that that letter grieved you, though only for a while.

There are some behaviors that a leader will use to demonstrate discipleship.

The leader will:

• Provide feedback to others for average and above average performance on a specific task
• Officially cite or recognize others for their accomplishments
• Provide feedback to subordinates on inappropriate, behavior, or performance
• Hold a subordinate accountable and disciplines appropriately

As a leader, you will be required to give feedback to others about their performance on the job. It is important feedback that will be helpful to them. For

---

[60] Frank Damazio, *The Making of a Leader* (Portland, Oregon: Bible Press, 1980), pp. 144-45.

[61] Blanchard, *The One Minute Manager*, p. 39.

you to give the most effective performance feedback to another person, keep the following five guidelines in mind.

1. Describe their behavior, not how you felt about what they did. Tell the person what he or she did by citing actual examples of behavior.

2. Be specific. The behavior demonstrated should be related to a standard or expectation that they are aware of.

3. Make the feedback useful. Give feedback that guides the individual in the process of improving.

4. Make the feedback timely. Provide performance feedback as close as possible to when the action occurs so that the individual receiving the feedback is most clearly able to relate to and understand his or her behavior.

5. Be fair and straightforward. Overloading a person with criticism or being overly nice colors the feedback and does not allow the person to get a true picture of his or her behavior. It is best if you are simply fair and straightforward and stick to the facts.

5. Disciples by training and developing others

The final task a leader must perform is what the Bible calls *discipleship*. Discipleship is the act of training and developing someone else. It is helpful for a leader to approach discipleship with the idea that the intent is to train his or her replacement. What does the other person need in order to move to do your job?

Don referenced a passage of Scripture, Matthew 20:18-20, that commands believers to use this skill to train others to be believers. To Christians this section of the Bible is called the Great Commission. It was significance to followers of Jesus because it is the last recorded personal instruction given by Him to His followers. It is also a special directive from Jesus to all of His followers to take specific action while on this earth.

And Jesus came and said to them, "All authority in heaven and on earth has been given to me. Go therefore and make disciples of all nations, baptizing them in the name of the Father and of the Son and of the Holy Spirit, teaching them to observe all that I have commanded you. And behold, I am with you always, to the end of the age."

Jesus starts off this session by giving the followers authority. When you delegate, it is key to delegate authority along with responsibility. If a leader gives a subordinate responsibility to complete a task without the authority to get it done, then the leader has delegated ineffectively. There are several verbs Jesus uses when He is telling his followers what to do, but the only imperative verb is "make disciples." An imperative verb is a command. We would probably put an exclamation point after a sentence containing an imperative command. That means making disciples, training and developing others is important in the Christian community. Leaders can learn from this. It is important for leaders to either directly or indirectly train their subordinates.

Throughout this book, reference has been made to John Maxwell's 2011 book, *The 5 Levels of Leadership*. The three drives people have and their subsequent leadership styles tie into the levels of leadership in his book. However, we have only referenced the first three levels until now. The fourth level of leadership, according to Maxwell, is People Development.[62] A level four leader is one who is training their replacement. An effective leader needs to be developing others in the tasks and job at hand, but also teaching others the leadership principles they have learned in this book. Isn't this what Don was doing with his subordinate, Mitch, in this story?

One example of this type of mentoring is found in the Bible in the books of 1 and 2 Kings.

Elijah finds his disciple in 1 Kings 19:19-21,

So he departed from there and found Elisha the son of Shaphat, who was plowing with twelve yoke of oxen in front of him, and he was with the twelfth. Elijah passed by him and cast his cloak upon him. And he left the oxen and ran after Elijah and said, "Let me kiss my father and my mother, and then I will follow you." And he said to him, "Go back again, for what have I done to you?" And he returned from following him and took the yoke of oxen and sacrificed them and boiled their flesh with the yokes of the oxen and gave it to the people, and they ate. Then he arose and went after Elijah and assisted him.

---

[62] John C. Maxwell, *The 5 Levels of Leadership*, p. 181.

Elijah served God for 10 years before He would send him a replacement to train, Elisha. Then Elijah would spend nearly the next 10 years training him. In 2 Kings 2:9-14, we see Elisha pick up the mantle from Elijah—literally. Elijah is ready to be replaced. He has taught his subordinate everything he knows. Now it is his time to do the work.

When they had crossed, Elijah said to Elisha, "Ask what I shall do for you, before I am taken from you." And Elisha said, "Please let there be a double portion of your spirit on me." And he said, "You have asked a hard thing; yet, if you see me as I am being taken from you, it shall be so for you, but if you do not see me, it shall not be so." And as they still went on and talked, behold, chariots of fire and horses of fire separated the two of them. And Elijah went up by a whirlwind into heaven. And Elisha saw it and he cried, "My father, my father! The chariots of Israel and its horsemen!" And he saw him no more.

Then he took hold of his own clothes and tore them in two pieces. And he took up the cloak of Elijah that had fallen from him and went back and stood on the bank of the Jordan. Then he took the cloak of Elijah that had fallen from him and struck the water, saying, "Where is the Lord, the God of Elijah?" And when he had struck the water, the water was parted to the one side and to the other, and Elisha went over.

There were many lessons Elijah poured into Elisha involving Ahab, the brook Cherith, the widow at Zarephath, a dead child, the prophets of Baal, drought and rain, weariness in battle and feeling abandoned by God. Elijah called a hard working young man whose heart was prepared to go the distance.

Have you identified whom you should be training? As you grow and develop as a leader, as you master the leadership styles and when they are appropriate, you then need to mentor other leaders to take up your mantle.

ABOUT THE AUTHOR

Daniel Blakeslee is an experienced public speaker, leader and a leadership coach. He is a Master Financial Coach, a pastor, college professor, husband and father. He coaches individuals who want to win with people and win with money. He has completed Dave Ramsey's,[63] Financial Coach Master Series Training.

Daniel lives with his wife, Michele, in Chesapeake, Virginia. He consults with non-profit organizations, churches and businesses to help them accomplish their mission efficiently and effectively.

Born and raised in Indianapolis, Indiana, Daniel enlisted in the U.S. Navy after graduating from high school. Daniel He entered the Submarine Service and advanced to Chief Petty Officer, serving on-board

---

[63] Completion of the Master Financial Coaching series training does not make him an employee or agent of Dave Ramsey, nor give him the right to speak for or bind Dave Ramsey, nor constitute an endorsement by Dave Ramsey or Ramsey Solutions.

three nuclear powered submarines as the Leading Engineering Laboratory Technician and an Engineering Watch Supervisor. Daniel was a highly decorated sailor, including four Navy Achievement Medals.

Before the first Gulf War, Daniel was assigned to the U.S. Navy's Leadership Development Program (NLDP) as an instructor. He taught hundreds of first-time managers and mentored them as they transitioned from worker to leader. He later joined the instructor school for the leadership program where officer and senior enlisted students consistently singled him out as a premiere instructor and leader. Daniel was awarded the Master Training Specialist for his work in the Leadership Instructor School.

Daniel developed curriculum for the pilot course for the Navy's Total Quality Management (TQM) Program. He designed the curriculum and taught the pilot course before he deployed in support of Operation Desert Storm.

Daniel served as the Lead Pastor and Executive Pastor of four churches. He was the Director of Operations for the Baptist Bible Fellowship International and on the faculty and administration of Baptist Bible College and Graduate School. He is currently serving as a pastor at the Point Harbor Community Church in Chesapeake, Virginia.

Riding his Harley Davidson motorcycle is Daniel's favorite pastime, but he escapes from strait jackets for fun. He actively speaks for groups, large and small, on the subject of leadership. He might even perform some illusions if you ask.

To schedule Daniel Blakeslee for your event call 800.326.8761 or visit www.blakeslee.com/speaking.

ADDITIONAL RESOURCES

Daniel's Blog
www.DanielBlakeslee.com

Leadership Style Survey
www.Blakeslee.com/leadershipstyles

Lead like Hell is Real
www.LeadLikeHellisReal.com

The Leader Code
www.TheLeaderCode.Com

Lead on Purpose
www.LeadonPurpose.org

Facebook.com/DanielBlakeslee

Twitter.com/DanielBlakeslee

Made in the USA
Charleston, SC
17 March 2015